BE NOT
TROUBLED

"Fr. Kirby shows himself to be a gentle but experienced spiritual director in the pages of *Be Not Troubled*. He guides the reader through the little-known but rich content of the French Jesuit Fr. Jean-Pierre de Caussade, who preached the radical notion of truly abandoning ourselves to God's will to find peace and joy. Packed with everyday wisdom and tips, Fr. Kirby's book reminds us of the many ways that God is with each of us through all of life's trials and tumult and that even in the midst of pain, suffering, and confusion, we can know God's love and will for our lives."

Carrie Gress
Author of *The Marian Option*

"It hurts to admit it, but I wasted many years worrying about the future. Through the writings of Fr. Jean-Pierre de Caussade, I discovered that my anxiety was caused by a failure to trust in God's providence. In *Be Not Troubled*, Fr. Jeff Kirby totally surprised me by presenting the teachings of Fr. Caussade in a fresh and practical way. This book is the perfect cure for troubled minds."

Gary Zimak
Author of *Give Up Worry for Lent!*

BE NOT TROUBLED

A 6-DAY PERSONAL RETREAT WITH
FR. JEAN-PIERRE DE CAUSSADE

Jeffrey Kirby

Based on the Spiritual Classic
Abandonment to Divine Providence

AVE MARIA PRESS AVE Notre Dame, Indiana

© 2019 by Jeffrey Kirby

All rights reserved. No part of this book may be used or reproduced in any manner whatsoever, except in the case of reprints in the context of reviews, without written permission from Ave Maria Press®, Inc., P.O. Box 428, Notre Dame, IN 46556, 1-800-282-1865.

Founded in 1865, Ave Maria Press is a ministry of the United States Province of Holy Cross.

www.avemariapress.com

Paperback: ISBN-13 978-1-59471-873-1

E-book: ISBN-13 978-1-59471-874-8

Cover image © Buena Vista Images/Getty Images.

Cover illustration by Samantha Watson.

Cover and text design by Katherine J. Ross.

Printed and bound in the United States of America.

Library of Congress Cataloging-in-Publication Data is available.

To
Dave and Julie Vasquez,
coworkers of the truth

Contents

Introduction

INVITATION TO PEACE

Thank you for picking up this book! Are you ready for an amazing six-day journey? I hope so, because you are in for a great spiritual treat. Yes, this book can help you. It is not about distant meditations or abstract principles. Life's too hard and too short for that approach. Instead, this book is written as an eminently practical guide and workable resource to help you truly find, or see more clearly, God's presence in your life. It will walk you through six days of reflections and resolutions based on the masterpiece *Abandonment to Divine Providence* by Fr. Jean-Pierre de Caussade.

With the inspiration from this spiritual master, the book's sole purpose is to help you relish God's goodness and his care for you, so that you will not be troubled—so that you might find peace. You will know that whatever is happening in your life, wherever you might be, or whatever sorrow God is allowing in your life, you are not alone. This book can help you to recognize God's presence.

SPIRITUAL MASTER AND MENTOR

In seeing the name of Fr. Jean-Pierre de Caussade, you might wonder, "Father who?" Admittedly, Jean-Pierre de Caussade is not a household name, and he is not one of the more prominent figures in our spiritual tradition. However, he has a story to tell, and his theological writings have given us an invaluable contribution to our understanding of divine providence, which is simply God's work in us and our lives. So who is Fr. Caussade, and why should we care about his classic, *Abandonment to Divine Providence*?

While not much is known about his life, from what we do know, we can see that he lived the message he taught. As a young man in the seventeenth century, he joined the Society of Jesus (now commonly called the Jesuits), which was a relatively new religious order at the time. Founded by St. Ignatius of Loyola, the order was committed to both a series of meditations called the Spiritual Exercises and to the Church's missionary mandate in the world. This was the balance of prayer and action that is reflected in Fr. Caussade's life and writings.

Among his duties as a Jesuit, Fr. Caussade was assigned to be the chaplain to the Visitation nuns in Nancy, France. During his time with them, he led various spiritual conferences. The sisters were so moved by his spiritual wisdom and practical guidance that they began to take notes during his talks and retained them within their community. Fr. Caussade never intended to write a book, and he would never have guessed that his notes would one day become a spiritual masterpiece. Yet the good sisters cherished Fr. Caussade's notes, and one hundred years later they saw to their publication under the title *Abandonment to Divine Providence*.

This is the spiritual masterpiece that we will be mining in order to hear Fr. Caussade's instructions and feel his encouragement in our own spiritual journey. It is important for us to remember that the notes-turned-book was written by a spiritual father and fellow companion along life's journey. He wrote it from a heartfelt desire to teach us the ways of God and to show us how to discern and recognize the divine presence in the world today.

Some friends in college introduced me to Fr. Caussade and the masterpiece *Abandonment to Divine Providence*. In a similar act of friendship, I would like to introduce him and his spiritual work to you.

Honestly, the first time I read *Abandonment to Divine Providence*, I was confused. I was not sure what the holy priest was trying to teach, and I was not in a good place to receive it. His counsel seemed shrouded in the scholastic language and French culture of his time. Later, as I suffered my own struggles in life, I picked up the work again. Surprisingly, I found Fr. Caussade to be like the consolation we feel in meeting up with an old friend we have not seen in a while. Suddenly I found his wisdom to be quickly relevant and comforting. For example, the holy priest gives the hopeful message that submission to God's will can change all occupations, troubles, and sufferings into divine gold.

In slowly rereading *Abandonment to Divine Providence*, I discovered Fr. Caussade to be an enlightening mentor in the spiritual life, particularly when it comes to maintaining a supernatural worldview in the midst of hurt and doubt.

The work became for me a source of perseverance and a cause of hope. Its spiritual truths are a cherished balm to the sufferings and anguish of life. But how could this seventeenth-century French priest understand me so well? How could his teachings touch me so deeply?

These questions, and many others like them, will be tackled in this book. Led by such questions, together we will glean the wealth of Fr. Caussade's wisdom. We will look into the ways of applying this treasury to our own lives so that we can grow spiritually and become firm believers in God and his presence among us.

ROLLING UP OUR SLEEVES

As we desire to move from youthful innocence to spiritual maturity, from sweetened milk to choice wine, childish views and quick fixes will not satisfy us. Cookie-cutter answers will fall flat. Images of God as some type of fairy godmother, who is oblivious to real sorrow and surrounded by nauseating optimism, will no longer adequately address the heartbreaking sufferings of our lives. Other self-delusions and fantasies that deny the real world and its fallenness will not help us understand our lives or see God's divine providence in their trenches.

We need something more, something deeper. We have to do the hard work of challenging our beliefs with the real sufferings of life, seeking active guidance, laboring to receive mature and sustainable answers from God, and then generously submitting to the God who loves us.

As we continue our journey by removing unhelpful idols, we now have to persevere and push ourselves to believe not only in God's existence but also truly *in* him. To fully believe *in* God means that we are willing to toil to see God's goodness and kindness in the darkness, emptiness, and uncertainty of life.

And so, dear reader, you know the starkness of the process described above and the hard work it involves. You have picked up this book because easy answers have not satisfied, and you are looking for something more. For me, in my journey, I have found the witness and writings of Fr. Jean-Pierre de Caussade to be a sure guide in discerning real, substantial answers to the deep questions and complicated realities of life. And now I have the privilege of introducing him to you. It is my hope that you will find Fr. Caussade as helpful a guide and as cherished a source of consolation as I have in my own spiritual journey.

A HELPFUL OUTLINE

When the notes of Fr. Caussade were compiled, they were divided into two major sections, simply titled "Book One," subdivided into two chapters, and "Book Two," subdivided into four chapters.

"Book One" consists of Fr. Caussade's foundational teachings, while "Book Two" is a more practical guide. In other words, we could compare "Book One" to a stage and backdrop, while "Book Two" is the script and the acting. Fully appreciating "Book One" in this way allows "Book Two" to build upon its foundation and open our hearts and minds to see and surrender to divine providence.

As we move through Fr. Caussade's *Abandonment to Divine Providence*, each of the chapters of the book forms a respective "day" of our six-day retreat.

Each day of the retreat could be as long or as short as you need (or want). As an initial expectation, perhaps you could block out about twenty-five minutes for each day. This will allow you time to read the day's wisdom, pray, reflect on how it pertains to the situations of your own life, and then consider some resolutions for your day and life in God. But any day of the retreat can be longer or shorter. My general counsel: go for as long as God is leading you!

In terms of when and how you might make our six-day retreat, here are a few options:

1. Start on a Monday and do the retreat for a week, concluding on a Saturday and then crowning the retreat with Sunday worship.
2. Devote a set day of the week, maybe Sunday, and make the retreat for six weeks. This could work well for special seasons, such as Lent or Advent, or for significant events in

your life, such as engagement for marriage, pregnancy, while grieving the loss of a loved one, and so on.

3. Take the six days and merge them into a two-day retreat while away on holiday or on a staycation. Read one day's wisdom for each point in the day: morning, noon, and evening.

These are only three suggestions out of many possibilities. The main point is to do the six-day retreat at the best time and in the best way for you.

Each of our chapters, or "days," bears the same title as the corresponding chapter in Fr. Caussade's work. It is my hope that this pairing will help us understand the original work. While the titles match, Fr. Caussade regularly floats his main themes throughout his different chapters (which match their original genres as verbally given retreat conferences). Many times, our esteemed author recalls and repeats lessons or insights here and there, and so this book does the same. One point might be found in more than one day's wisdom.

On each day of this retreat, you will be invited to participate in the following:

1. Opening Invitation: Each day will begin with an invitation to us to enter into the presence of God.
2. Teaching: We will explore Fr. Caussade's wisdom and slowly unlock the treasury of the spiritual classic. This part will be our central focus as we lay out Fr. Caussade's truths, insights, and counsel.

3. Spiritual Steps: Having laid out the treasures before us, we will conclude the day with a list of suggested practical acts that are meant to guide us in applying Fr. Caussade's teachings.
4. Closing Prayer: Last, I will offer a concluding prayer to help us redirect our spiritual energies and make active resolutions toward God and our neighbor.

Each of these different parts of our six days is intended to direct and encourage us along the way. As we journey, we will explore and wrestle with the truths presented by Fr. Caussade, and we will learn how to see God's presence more brightly in our lives and surrender more willingly and joyfully to his divine providence.

Let's begin. And as we do so, let's keep the eyes of our hearts open! Let's be aware of God's presence and remember his goodness that is always among us, around us, and within us.

And so suspend the skepticism and quietism, dispel the doubt and despair, temper the negativity and cynicism, open the wounds, convert the anger, and reform the jealousy and envy. Repent. Turn around and recognize the kingdom of God. Hear the lessons of Fr. Caussade, our spiritual master and mentor, who toils to show us his own lived experience of God, who generously passes on his lessons of the spiritual life, and who seeks to disclose the face of God to each of us in our own lives today.

On Doing Our Part and Leaving the Rest to God

OPENING INVITATION

- Set aside your worries of the day.
- Take some deep breaths. Invite God into your day.
- Ask God to speak to you through this day's wisdom.
- Begin when you are ready!

A FATHER'S WITNESS

I was not sure what was happening. I was sleeping soundly as only a child could. The rain was gently tapping on my windowpane. My father arrived home unexpectedly from military maneuvers. He was shaking me and yelling for my siblings to get up. He was still in his battle dress uniform, and it was muddy. He was crying. I was very confused—my father always had a well-pressed, pristine uniform, and he rarely cried. As I entered the bright living room, I tried to adjust my eyes to the light as

I watched my dad pace the floor. He was distracted, and kept calling my siblings to hurry up. My mom was already up. She was sitting in a chair with a look of disbelief on her face and her arms crossed, as if comforting herself. As my discomfort grew, I wondered, "What's going on? What's happening? Is everything all right?"

After all of us crowded into the living room, my father just stared at us. He was so upset. He tried to talk, but his voice kept cracking and his tears kept flowing. He tried to compose himself but it took him some time. I was terrified. I wondered, "What is going on?"

After what seemed like forever for a child, my dad was able to speak, and he told us about the accident. Earlier that evening during a convoy in severe rain, a vehicle lost control, slid off the road, and overturned. In the pandemonium, a young soldier was thrown around the vehicle and banged his head. It would be a mortal wound. My father was the first on the scene. He found the soldier—whom he knew, who had his whole life ahead of him—in great pain.

We had welcomed this young man into our home for many a holiday meal. I remembered him as a very skinny African American man with a little acne. He was shy and would not go for seconds, and so my mom was always filling his plate. It was clear by his demeanor that he thought the world of my father, and he always spoke to him with respect. This particular soldier was only four years older than my brother.

Arriving at the scene of the accident, my father attempted first response procedures but to no avail. He held the young man in his arms as he died. As medical personnel arrived, my father would not let go. The lifeless body had to be slowly pried from his arms, and he was given permission to return home.

As my father told us the story, it was obvious he was deeply troubled by the experience. He explained that he needed to wake us up to know that we were OK. After telling us this story, my father was overcome with emotion and started to cry again. He gathered us up in his strong arms and hugged us. He would not let us go. This was the first time I remember my father being so affectionate.

I had never heard anything like this story before, and the tragedy of this fallen soldier rocked my world. Seeing my father so broken shook everything I knew. How was I supposed to understand tragedy and sorrow? "Is anything safe?" I wondered.

This was my first glimpse into the harsh reality of life. Although I grew up on an army base in Cold War West Germany, my parents fostered a warm and loving environment and kept the tension and uncertainty of the Cold War at bay. My siblings and I, along with our friends on the military base, lived a relatively normal childhood.

It seemed my father was always on training maneuvers, especially after President Ronald Reagan's 1987 visit in which he challenged the Soviet leader, "Mr. Gorbachev, tear down this wall." The military operations never seemed out of the ordinary, and my dad being away was just the way things were. The fathers of all my friends were also away and, as kids, we were distant from world affairs. We were more worried about preadolescent pimples, what shoes to wear, where to sit on the bus, and how to escape embarrassing moments in class.

On that training operation, however, a soldier died. The only time the innocence of my world was broken was when that solider died. How could a child understand what that meant? How could any sense be made of it? Over the following days I watched my father prepare a letter to the soldier's family, and this unenviable task tore him up.

I remember asking him with a child's level of compassion, "Dad, what are you going to write? How are you going to explain it?" Surprisingly, my father actually smiled at my questions, as if they reminded him of a secret weapon. He unbuttoned the chest pocket of his uniform and pulled out a small green book, a beat-up old copy of the New Testament. He flipped to a dog-eared page and read to me:

> Do not let your hearts be troubled. Believe in God, believe also in me. In my Father's house there are many dwelling places. If it were not so, would I have told you that I go to prepare a place for you? And if I go and prepare a place for you, I will come again and will take you to myself, so that where I am, there you may be also. And you know the way to the place where I am going. (Jn 14:1–4)

After reading the biblical passage, my father looked at me and explained, "You see, Jeff, God is taking care of things. We just have to trust him."

This was a memorable experience for me, because my father is a quiet disciple. Honestly, I think this was the first time he opened up to me and spontaneously shared his faith. In receiving this unexpected but timely testimony, I was able to see that as I trusted in my father, so he was confident in the Heavenly Father. And so my dad's answer was an inspiring witness to me of what I would later call trusting in divine providence.

DIVINE PROVIDENCE

Admittedly, we might hear this expression and wonder what *divine providence* means. My father did not know, and he would not have used that term. My use of it came later, from a different father in the spiritual realm. For me at that point, divine providence was a vague notion that God was in charge, and even if bad things happened, we could trust him because everything would be all right.

My father's reliance on God pointed me to the loving-kindness of the Almighty and showed me a path to discern his genuine care for us and for our world. My father never had the opportunity to read theological or spiritual works, and so as I mentioned, he would not have used terms such as *providence* or expressions such as *passive will* or *sacrament of the present moment*. And I am sure he never heard of the spiritual father

Jean-Pierre de Caussade. My father just knew of God's presence and compassion within and throughout the twists and turns of life. He actively performed the duties of his vocation as husband, father, and soldier, and attentively served God, his country, and his beloved family.

And so my father gave me a life-changing glimpse into divine providence. By unveiling it, he showed me his way in approaching the ambiguities, sufferings, and sorrows of life. He taught me his secret to persevering through the joys, comforts, tragedies, and losses of life.

PEACEFUL BALM AND BALANCED ANSWER

Into any time of uncertainty or distress, the message of divine providence is a contradiction. We are called to both submission and action. Interior peace comes when we focus on the joy of surrendering to divine providence while both living and acting in the present moment. All people of good will are summoned to contemplation and to activity. This counsel of trust and abandonment to God's goodness, which has been firetested and proven in the lives of countless holy ones throughout the ages, is offered to each of us today. In the arena of our own worries and perplexities, we are shown a more excellent way, namely, the love of God and of our neighbor.

This message offers to calm our restlessness by directing our hearts. It reminds us of God's love and care for us, and gives us a liberating wisdom that dispels anxiety and isolationism as it opens widely a door to us to both interior peace and the selfless performance of our duties in life.

In many respects, the message of God's providence pulls away the veil of our illusions and calls us to reality. It guides us to step back and see the whole panorama of existence. As we look, we see goodness and beauty, but also evil and suffering. "But why the darkness?" we might ask. Our minds could speculate: "If God is all-powerful and all-good, how could there possibly be wickedness and sorrow in our world? With the presence of evil, it would seem that God is either not all-powerful, since he cannot stop it; or he is not all-good, since he could prevent it but chooses not to." With this argument volleying in our minds, we see two extremes.

One response could be atheism. In witnessing rampant hurt and gloom, we could throw up our hands and quit on God, believing that either he does not exist or that he has failed us. This type of anti-theism is motivated by a belief that, since God is absent or negligent, we have to take up the work and build our own kingdom of man. And so we have to either join or fight evil for ourselves. If we are honest, there are times or extreme moments when we have all heard this option whisper to our hearts: "God, where are you? Are you real? Don't you care?"

Another response to our sober inquiry could be quietism. In being scandalized by villainy and depravity, we could spiritually succumb to its influence and accept the false conviction that life is evil, and we could give up on the capacity or possibility of goodness. We could assume maliciousness is the norm. We could choose to completely remove ourselves from life, isolate ourselves from reality, and deny the power of any activity other than that within our own souls. Again, this drive—to shut out the world, deny life, and put our souls on lockdown—is also a tempting whisper in turbulent or distressing times: "God, why have you left? Why is there so much evil? Am I to be alone in my own soul?"

Both of these options are possibilities and yet neither one is real. Neither satisfies our hearts or fulfills the generous invitation to surrender to divine providence. Each one is an escape, a well-devised hiding place that robs us of the mystery of life and all its richness, grace, and glory. Breaking through these misguided, cowardly, and weak options, we are offered a middle way. We are presented with the option of both *submission* and *action*. Let's explore this.

We begin by asserting that the world and human life are fundamentally good. Evil happens, and it can be daunting. It is agonizing to our souls. We can react and want to get away. We desperately seek a balm to soothe our souls. Without reflection, we can either be assimilated into atheistic action with overly busy lives or escape by enclosing ourselves in layers of inertia. Faith will have none of these options. It holds our hands to the fire. Faith unmasks the immaturity of both options. It demands self-reflection, examination, and integrity.

Faith calls us to ask questions and labor for answers. It proposes a different perspective and points us along a different path. Evil does happen, but it does not have the last word. Creation is good. The wickedness may run rampant in the Garden, but the Garden is still good and can still bear good fruit. Yes, the world is fallen, humanity is free and sinful, and bad things happen, but divine providence is able to bring all things to a good end for those who love God (see Romans 8:28).

Yes, this is our world after the Fall from grace contained in the biblical story of the Garden of Eden, but wickedness does not have an everlasting force, and it is not the basis of who we are or what our world was created to be. Each of us, and the world in which we live, is good. In spite of evil and suffering, we are blessed and cherished by a loving God, who is among us and bears all things with us.

Yet God does permit evil to happen because he respects our freedom. He also allows the wayward flow and fallenness of creation. But any wickedness that is permitted by his passive will—either of the moral or natural order—only has the power we give it. God ennobles us with the wisdom and glory to vanquish the kingdom of sin and death, to be free, and to dwell in peace. And so to those who draw close to him, God brings about an even greater good from any evil. Depravity is destroyed by bold and daring goodness.

This is the divine action that calls for our submission. It is this action that radically motivates people of good will to work energetically and tirelessly to dismantle darkness, suffer persecution for righteousness, and generously extend themselves in the service of others so that light can dispel gloom and iniquity from every corner of the world. By working for goodness against the evil that is permitted through God's passive will, we show our belief in divine providence and manifest God's desire for righteousness throughout creation. It is a providence that places every suffering and sorrow within an everlasting and magnanimous horizon. It reveals to us the true identity of creation and humanity, beloved by God.

This is the loving union of God and humanity that is bypassed in the self-absorption of the quietist and denied in the empty activism of the atheist. We are called to something more and something greater. Faith points the way and describes for us the freedom and joy that is found in an unconditional surrender to divine providence.

And so we are helped in our discernment of God's providence. Faith gives us a stronger conviction of the divine presence and action among us. It shows us God's power and healing strength. It displays his abundant goodness to such an extent that we wish to become instruments of that same goodness in our world today.

What will you do with this holy testimony? Will you ignore it and leave divine providence behind, or try to create your own providence by a faulty belief in yourself? Or will you truly surrender? The invitation is offered. The choice is yours.

SPIRITUAL STEPS

Some practical thoughts to help us all live the wisdom of divine providence:

- As you are preparing yourself for the day, ask God to help you see his providence in your life today.
- Pause during an activity or take a brief walk in the middle of the day. Reflect on what has already happened and what is still to come. Ask "What is God's message for this day?"
- As you prepare for bed, examine your day and note where you noticed God's presence. Thank him for those moments. If you did not experience God's presence today, express this in prayer to God and ask for the graces to see him tomorrow.

CLOSING PRAYER

Good and gracious God,
I turn to you, abandoning myself to your providence.
Please show me the way.
Show me your goodness and manifest your care to me.
Lord, I want to cooperate with you and see you
in all that I do.
I consecrate my every moment
and all my duties to you.
Lord, draw close to me.
Grant me consolation and perseverance.
Bestow your peace upon me.
Help me to always dwell in your providence.
I make this prayer through Jesus Christ,
who is Lord, forever and ever.
Amen.

Embrace the Present Moment as an Ever-Flowing Source of Holiness

OPENING INVITATION

- Set aside your worries of the day.
- Take some deep breaths. Invite God into your day.
- Ask God to speak to you through this day's wisdom.
- Begin when you are ready!

TWO DIFFERENT BUT SIMILAR WORLDS

At first glance, our contemporary culture seems very different from the world of Fr. Caussade's seventeenth-century France, but the two have some notable similarities. For starters, the endeavor to surrender to divine providence is never an easy achievement, regardless of the culture or century. Our fallen minds are darkened by vanity, seduced by illusions of control, and attracted to drama and the passing things of this world. We can be distrustful, spiritually murky, and inclined to distraction. This is human nature, and it has not changed much over the centuries.

In Western culture today, we always want to be in the know. We refuse to fully participate in life because we anticipate it with an obsessive desire for control. We are easily enchanted with shows and spectacles, stimulated by excessive activity, ravished by commotion, and overly excited by empty thrills. Above all, we avoid divine providence in the present moment because it requires honesty about who we are, and it calls for a transformation toward what we are called to be. In this existential circus, if we do not make ourselves a living sacrifice to the present moment, then we can easily lose ourselves. If we would only lift the veil and watch with vigilant attention, God would endlessly reveal himself to us.

Yes, the pace of Western culture is fueled by the famed convictions of FOMO (Fear of Missing Out) and YOLO (You Only Live Once). These cultural slogans showcase a fever-pitch intensity that demands high levels of attention, focus, and juggling of duties, ambitions, and follow-ups.

The goal of such activity is to be always present in some way, shape, or form in several places at once. You could be talking to your mother on the phone, completing work projects, watching television, eating a snack, checking social media, responding to a text, and mentally reviewing your to-do list for later in the day. And this could be a light day! We have so much going on in so many different locales and in so many different types of media. We are stretched to our limits.

The velocity caused by such a high level of multitasking can lead us to forget who we are or where we truly want to be. We can neglect sacred things—the worship of God, prayer—and let important things—marriage, family, other relationships—be eclipsed by the constant flow of seemingly urgent things. In this shuffle, the real treasures of our lives can get lost along the way. We get caught up in the overall rat race that empties our lives of their meaning. The hustle-bustle might temporarily satisfy us with its drama, creature comforts, or personal successes, but we are ultimately left wanting something more.

This is our world today. Does Fr. Caussade's world have any resemblance to it? Can his wisdom be applied to our experience today in the twenty-first century?

While Fr. Caussade's state of affairs was different, it bore striking spiritual similarities to our own. The world of our blessed author was marked by religious anxiety, conflicting loyalties, and social stress. After decades of religious wars, the delicate peace established between Catholics and Protestants always seemed to be on the breaking point, with a return to arms and violence as a real possibility.

In order to maintain that peace, some writers called people to complete inactivity, a system of thought that has come to be called quietism. The quietists endorsed a complete removal from any type of involvement or course of action in life. It was defeatist, self-centered, and overall extremely unhelpful to spreading God's kingdom in people's hearts and in the world. This was not the solution proposed by Fr. Caussade. He points us in a different direction.

OUR MENTOR'S CHALLENGE

Admittedly, *Abandonment to Divine Providence* is not for the fainthearted. If life has remained for you a world of rainbows and butterflies, then this spiritual classic is not for you right now. If, however, you have experienced hurt, harm, confusion, sufferings, and sorrows of this life, then the writings of Fr. Caussade can help. You will find him to be a welcomed relief and source of hope.

The work of our blessed author is written for those who welcome the Cross, or at least have stopped trying to circumvent it. The masterpiece is a challenge. It demands that we search for value, purpose, and meaning in the array of our human experience—from tragedy and joy to darkness and light. It is an aid to each of us to completely surrender to the workings of divine providence as a mixture of faith, hope, and love, which unites us to God and his work among us.

In this effort, we must not be cowardly, but generous and bold. As we nurture this generosity of heart, let's continue our journey.

GROWING INTO IT

After the witness from my father, I continued to watch him and saw his reliance on divine providence play out in a thousand different scenarios. This formation provided me with a strong foundation for my own faith.

My father's witness, matched by my mother's own testimony, laid a foundation for me, but I needed to grow into my own belief in divine providence. I had to build on this foundation and accept this truth as my own. All things considered, my parents protected me and my siblings from a lot of danger, anxiety, and distress. In that carefree world, it was easy to accept my parents' faith and follow their lead. But as with all children, I needed to grow up. In my adulthood, I had to stand on my own two feet, roll up my sleeves, and build upon the foundation given to me by my parents' generous faith.

As things turned out, the verses following the biblical passage quoted by my father shed some light:

> Thomas said to him, "Lord, we do not know where you are going. How can we know the way?" Jesus said to him, "I am the way, and the truth, and the life. No one comes to the Father except through me." (Jn 14:5–6)

In the passage, St. Thomas the Apostle is posing his own query and trying to come to a greater awareness of what the Lord Jesus was saying to him. The apostle, later called "Doubting Thomas" for questioning the Resurrection, was not going to accept easy answers or settle for cheap grace. He wanted to understand things for himself, and so he openly inquired. The Lord welcomed these exchanges and blessed Thomas. He rewarded the apostle's transparency and persistence and, by this approach, Thomas went through a deeper conversion and embraced the Lord's care for him. He chose to truly follow Jesus without reservation because he found good answers to his hard questions. This led him to preach the Gospel without fear and to die as a holy martyr in India.

Like St. Thomas, my father, and all those who desire pure hearts before God, we have to ask our own questions. More specifically, we have to push ourselves and inquire within our own souls: "Do I believe in divine providence? Will I surrender my life to this truth?"

These are the sorts of questions I started to encounter as I moved away from my family and started college. I began to face my own sufferings, watch my own life be rocked by agonies and sorrows, struggle to keep things together, and try to understand various heartaches of my own.

In choosing a college, I decided on a small Catholic liberal arts college in Ohio. If I had stayed in my own home state, my education would have been covered and I would have even made a little money. I passed on state-based scholarships and grants and chose a Catholic institution. The tuition was burdensome. I had to work several jobs and every dollar counted. There were times when I did not know whether I would be able to financially afford the next semester. There just was not enough money for comfort. I struggled with this reality: "How is there not enough money? I'm trying to attend a Catholic college and get an education—why doesn't God help me? Where is divine providence?"

Entering college was a time for new beginnings and new friends. Leaving a close-knit family and finding people to love and care about beyond a family connection was not as simple as I expected. Some people did not like me, my personality, or my views. What? Others were too busy or already had a social network and did not want more vulnerability or responsibility. Why? A few had a limited sense of trust or benevolence and could not have deep friendships. How come? Meanwhile, there were others who were kind and wanted to figure out what having close friendships beyond family really meant. But the whole experience was a mixed bag. It never seemed consistent. Everything was changing. People were changing, and friendships were up and down. "Why is this so difficult? I just want to be a friend and have friends. Shouldn't love and caring for others be easy? Where is divine providence?"

Within broader friendships, there were unsettling questions about dating and affection. Questions ranged from "How do I know if an attraction is being returned?" to "What does it mean to be someone's boyfriend?" to "Why are my personal values, my care for others, and my emotions and sexual desires all getting jumbled up and confused?" The distinction between love and lust, selflessness and self-centeredness, and the expectations I had of myself and my actual actions all crashed into each other, blurred, and caused a lot of anxiety in my heart: "Why is this so complicated? Shouldn't virtue and character always win? Where is divine providence?"

While in college, my grandfather died. He was a man with a questionable narrative, who hurt and caused harm to many people. My family could never invite him to be a part of our life and, even at his death, there was no reconciliation between him and my father. The death was regrettably uneventful and isolated. There were no tears, no heartfelt conversations, no apologies, no joy. He just died without a happy ending. But I thought there were supposed to be conversions, warm exchanges, wonderful reconciliations, and a spirit of joyful hope when someone died. But that was not the case. It was a quiet phone call, a long car drive, and a funeral service without grace or emotion. "How does this happen? I thought there are always supposed to be happy endings? Where is divine providence?"

These experiences are only four of many others that were growing pains for me as I sought to see and understand divine providence. Perhaps you have several of your own. For me, each one of these experiences posed a new question of God, raised an unexpected objection to his goodness, and led me at times to shake my fist to the heavens and declare, "This isn't fair! Why is this happening?"

Does this level of frustration have to win? Is this the only answer? Are we orphans, abandoned in the universe, with random pointless actions dismissed by a nonexistent or negligent deity?

THE INVITATION TO SURRENDER

In the midst of these experiences of suffering, confusion, and anxiety, divine providence reminds us that these experiences and dispositions of the soul do not need to have the last word. Unless we want to live in the cesspool, there is a way out. Faith points us to the mystery and beauty of God's providence and calls us to a radical surrender—from the depths of our hearts—to the workings of this divine providence.

Such an abandonment to divine providence is not a reliance on ourselves and our own strengths, or a trust in our own tenacity. It is also not a futile exercise in wishful thinking or fantasy. Our surrender is a broadening of our minds and hearts to the eternal and infinite. It is a willingness to look beyond the immediate sufferings or sorrows of our lives and to place them within the larger picture of existence and goodness. Our abandonment to divine providence is not a waiting game to get what we want, how we want it, and when we want it. Rather, it is a true surrender. We place our needs, wants, and hopes before God, here and now, and then we let go. We trust that God knows better, and so we accept—and even begin to desire—that the answers to our requests will be answered according to his infinite and loving plan.

Truly, abandonment to divine providence is not a concession to positivism, the belief that everything is determined solely by our own human power or by scientific research. Again, our surrender is not a ploy to get what we want. It is a true sacrifice of our will to the workings of divine providence. It is a sincere

trust in God that is willing to accept suffering and disappointment for a greater good. Our abandonment to divine providence
is the tough decision to live in the present moment and not in
future hopes or past hurts. It is a willingness to look and search
for God here and now, and not later or somewhere else. This is
the way of freedom, peace, and loving service.

In this way, the anger or bewilderment of life that can cause
us to shake our fists to the heavens, avoid prayer, or reject faith
is offered a different path. It is a path that is rich in meaning,
purpose, and value. It is the path of goodness and selflessness.

Will we choose this different path? Will we allow love and
goodness to have a voice and a part in the wrestling match for
the throne of our own hearts and of our world today?

SPIRITUAL STEPS

Some practical thoughts to help us all live the wisdom of divine
providence:

- What event or experience tempts you to live in the past?
  Turn to God and leave it in the past today. Find God's
  presence here and now.
- What anxiety or concern tempts you to live in the future?
  Entrust the future to God and find his goodness in your
  life here and now.
- Pause periodically throughout the day for a minute or two
  and pray, "Lord, I know you are here." Let yourself feel his
  presence with you.

CLOSING PRAYER

Eternal and living God,
I seek you in my life today, here in this place.
Show me your presence. Pour your grace into my heart.
Reveal your kindness and goodness to me.
Lord, I want to cooperate with you and see you
in all that I do.
Give me your strength.
Help me to search for you in difficulty, discern you in
darkness, and wait for you in sorrow.
Lord, be with me. Help me to always surrender to you.
Accompany me. Show me your presence
and way of love.
You are my joy in laughter and my triumph in hope.
Help me to always dwell in your providence.
I make this prayer through Jesus Christ,
who is Lord, forever and ever.
Amen.

To Surrender to God Is to Practice Every Virtue

OPENING INVITATION

- Set aside your worries of the day.
- Take some deep breaths. Invite God into your day.
- Ask God to speak to you through this day's wisdom.
- Begin when you are ready!

VIRTUE AND THE LIFE OF GRACE

In our culture today, we hear a lot about values. Each of us values something and this appreciation nurtures a set of values. While these are important in life, values are different from virtues. Rather than just flowing from our own hearts, virtues reflect an order of life outside of ourselves. This order of life is given by God, to which we are intimately bound as his beloved children. When we exercise virtue, we participate in this order of life, this living chain of existence and grace.

For example, when we tell the truth, not only because we personally value the truth but also because we recognize that telling the truth is something good in itself, then we participate in a goodness that is both outside of us and quickly becomes a part of us and helps us understand who we truly are as God's children.

Virtue, therefore, is the acknowledgment of God's will and our acceptance to do whatever he asks of us at a particular time, in a particular state of affairs, and in a particular way. This is important since one virtue might be right in one instance but wrong in another.

For example, justice and fortitude were needed by the leaders of the civil rights movement. If gentleness or humility had been exercised, they would not have been able to endure the hardship of their efforts and accomplish such noble conclusions. By contrast, if more temperance and compassion had been shown before the Iraq War, rather than zeal and fortitude, an international armed conflict may have been prevented.

Seen in this light, we can say that virtue is holiness in the moment. Virtue is a release of God's grace at a particular time and place. Understanding virtue in this way helps us understand how a surrender to divine providence is the beginning and seedbed of a life of virtue. By recognizing and graciously submitting to God's loving will in our lives, we open ourselves up to an array of virtues, goodness, and freedom.

Perhaps an example can help.

A FATHER'S WITNESS REVISITED

"Jeff, did you hear what's happening to me?" The question stung as much as the answer. I knew what my father was asking. My mother called earlier and told me about the doctor's visit. I was not sure if her first call was simply to let me know or a safe avenue for my mom to voice the truth and shed a few tears. No one was expecting this. Dad was too strong. But even robust and accomplished people such as my father still only have human minds and bodies like everyone else. They are still vulnerable.

My father was not perfect, and the world certainly did not revolve around him, but he always seemed to be on top of things. He was a bastion of strength and self-control. As kids, we called him "the mean green fighting machine" since he was always somewhat muscular, regularly in his green army uniform, and the model of precision and fortitude. Dad was tough, a type of cowboy and soldier all rolled into one. While it should not have, my mom's phone call completely caught me off guard.

The signs had all been there for about a year leading up to his appointment. My father would get easily frustrated over small things, which was unusual for him. His agitation would quickly escalate over ridiculous things such as not being able to get the dishes to fit in the dishwasher. He would suddenly lash out in anger at my mom when he could not work the remote control to turn on the television. This was completely out of character for him. Self-control was not only drummed into him as a soldier but also a value he tried to instill in his children.

He might lose his temper in the heat of the moment but it was always fair and tempered with justice.

Additionally, Dad began to stumble over easy words and repeat himself. He often appeared confused in areas of his expertise. He would get lost driving to well-known locations. But with each mishap or outburst, our family made excuses, sought reasons, and looked for solutions: He's really tired. Dad needs some rest. He's been working very hard. Dad needs to relax a little. He's getting old. Maybe it's time to retire. We would laugh and fill in the blanks. But as things got worse, our laughter stopped and our explanations sounded more and more strained. In my own heart I feared, "Is something wrong with Dad? Who am I trying to comfort, Dad or myself?"

My mom finally summoned up the courage to face reality and contacted the doctor. When it was time—for the first time in my memory—she drove my father to the hospital. She had never needed to drive my father before. He always drove the two of them. When she called me afterward, I knew it was not going to be good news. What was wrong with Dad? Although I should not have been, I was shocked and numb: "How is this possible? My father is too young and robust. My family needs him. How could this happen? Can we fix this? There must be some mistake. How will my mother cope?"

These questions and more were swirling in my heart when the phone rang again. I was not ready for this. I was still in shock. But my father's calm voice came through the phone and he sounded great. "Jeff, did you hear what's happening to me?"

It was such an honest and simple question, but the answer was an almost overwhelming mountain to cross. I could not talk, and I did not want to say the word "dementia." And so there was silence. Knowing my temperament, my father was patient and waited for me to answer. Eventually, with a crackling voice and pushed-back tears, I responded, "Yes, Dad, Mom told me. So it's dementia?" True to his own temperament, my father laughed and said, "Yeah, I'm losing my mind!" I could not laugh, and I could not hold back my tears anymore. I just started crying like I never have before.

It is unsettling to cry without control, and it is odd to cry with someone over the phone. It is just horrible to sob in the face of suffering from which there is no cure or treatment and will only get worse. I tried to stop; I labored to compose myself. I could not. My own soul was grieving heavily. Of course, my father let me cry.

As a priest I have sat with countless families in this same type of situation. My role is to be a stable presence and provide warm reassurances of God's divine providence. But this was different. This is my dad and I was just a hurting child of such a good man.

Eventually I had no tears left and there was a pause. My father, quiet up to this point, laughed again and casually said to me, "Jeff, this isn't a big deal. We'll get through this." This response brought an unexpected flash of anger, and without thinking I said, "No, Dad, this is a big deal. You're not supposed to get sick." He laughed again, repeating, "I'm not supposed to get sick? Who said that?" The reality stung. But it just was not fair! All his hard work for other people. His service to his family, our country, and to God. How could he not be spared something like this? Why couldn't he and my mother enjoy an active and happy retirement? They had earned it. Couldn't God have allowed something like this to bypass my father? How could this be happening?

My father's voice broke through the internal voices: "Jeff, we all get sick. We'll be all right." Always my father and always the one to point to divine providence in his own way, as he once showed me the verse, "Do not let your hearts be troubled" (Jn 14:1). Yes, this was my father pointing to God's plan and his goodness. Not misguided euphoria or self-delusion. No, he knew his illness and he knew its consequences, but he also knew a higher peace and he was showing me the way.

Truly, God's activity runs throughout the universe. It dwells all around us and penetrates each one of us. Wherever we are, there is God's activity. It moves ahead of us, it is within us, and it follows us. *All we have to do is recognize it and allow it to sweep over us.*

A CONTINUED JOURNEY

It has been almost two years since this conversation with my father. In that time, my family has adjusted to the ups and downs of this disease. There have been numerous doctors' appointments, tests and retests, medications and more medications, side effects and medications to treat the side effects. There have been dietary adjustments, financial difficulties, sleeping problems, and painful changes to family roles. My older brother has heroically put his own life on hold to help my mother care for my father.

It has not been an easy journey. While there have been outbursts of anger and heartaches, there have also been times of affection, heartfelt remembrances, humor, humility, and consoling grace. My father is consciously working to do his part and to leave the rest to God. He is actively struggling to live in the comfort of a belief in divine providence every day. It is this belief that has shaped his entire life and that has given him meaning and hope in every situation. He is a model of Christian witness for my entire family.

A WITNESS REVEALED

Watching my father face his disease with calm humility has been a rewarding and purifying experience for me. It is in the everyday details where I see his acceptance of God's providence and how this acceptance gives birth to an array of other virtues and good actions. Here is a man, a believer, who beautifully displays the wisdom of divine providence. Here is a life that exemplifies what the abandonment to divine providence looks like in the thick and thin of reality.

There have been several moving experiences that stand as penetrating reflections of my father's trust in divine providence and the virtues that flow from this surrender. These situations have served as strong lessons to me and my family of how an abandonment to God brings forth multiple other virtues wherever we might be or in whatever circumstance we might find ourselves.

THE VIRTUE OF SELFLESS SERVICE

My dad once led units of soldiers during the Cold War. After his retirement, he entered the private sector and directed the maintenance operations of a large factory. He treated each of his responsibilities, whether in the service or in the private sector, with the utmost deference and care. He was completely committed to his work. He knew each staff member and was attentive to their personal strengths and needs (and the needs of their families). He managed the factory operations with the same meticulous attention to detail as any military maneuver. When my father was on the job, his superiors could rest knowing that everything was under control.

He saw his duties as opportunities to serve God and the greater good, as well as to provide for his family. With dementia, however, he is unable to work outside of the home. However, he has created a new regimen of duties. Working with my mother, he brings the same exactitude to humbly sweeping the front steps, vacuuming the living room, and making up the bed.

These tasks might sound trivial to some, but my father takes these duties very seriously. Some may believe that such a diagnosis is license to think that a person with such a condition can make no contribution or that God is finished working with them. My father sees that his role has changed but his dedication to each of these smaller duties is still an integral part of my family's life and work. No condition or illness steals our dignity or eclipses our call to "do our part." Divine grace is found in every situation, even the simplest or most ordinary tasks, and the fulfillment of our duties is how we participate in this grace and share it with others. In his own modest way of going from commanding soldiers and supervising a factory to sweeping and vacuuming a house, my father knows that there is still work to be done and that he has a place.

THE VIRTUE OF FAITH

Faith gives my father a pat on the back as he teaches us that the best thing for us to do is found in the present moment. Once a moment passes, the will of God is now manifesting itself in new circumstances. It is in fulfilling each duty in the moment, no matter in what disguise it presents itself, that helps us to grow deeper in holiness.

Although my father would bark orders at distracted soldiers, reprimand incompetent staff, or discipline unruly children, he was always fair when he had to be firm. Now, however, he experiences bursts of frustration when he cannot remember people, places, details, or events. In these outbursts of raw anger, he visibly becomes a different person. After every such moment, he himself is shocked by his behavior and is filled with noticeable remorse and repentance. He is humbled by the loss of control and the darkness that is released.

THE VIRTUE OF HUMILITY

In these times, my father takes on a childlike innocence as he apologizes for his comments and seeks forgiveness for his offenses. He could hide behind a dozen excuses relating to his condition but instead he takes on a noble accountability and offers genuine apology. These actions are particularly heart-warming when they are extended to my mother, who is often the recipient of these outbursts but who loves him and offers him constant care. My father understands that "doing his part" includes real humility and accountability for his actions. He must continue to exercise other virtues such as kindness, compassion, and consistent self-control. For a man who has lived a life that has exemplified goodness, service, and self-reliance, it must be a particularly weighty cross for him to not only struggle to remember things but also to be kind to himself and others. When the fog of uncertainty will not let him remember and patience is lost, what meekness it must take for him to apologize and seek reconciliation.

Faith acclaims this way of life. It teaches that God's action is boundless in its scope and power, but it can only fill our souls if we empty them of all false confidence in our own abilities.

God can, when he pleases, change all other obstacles into aids for spiritual progress.

THE VIRTUES OF GENTLENESS AND HUMOR

Throughout my father's life, he approached various difficult situations with unexpected humor, and he continues to do so in the trials of his dementia. I suspect his lifelong reliance on divine providence has always made him comfortable in his own skin, in the struggles and sorrows of life, and in this fallen world. He knows that God is ultimately in control and so he is able to rest, find joy, and laugh at the passing things of this world. It seems to me that my father holds the conviction of divine providence as a type of secret weapon that can foil and destroy evil and convert suffering and sorrow into joy. And so to the surprise of my family and to many of our friends, my father has used humor to accept awkward moments that arise.

On one occasion, my sister was patiently reminding my dad of the plan for the day. My father kept mixing up the details and forgetting pertinent facts. She continued to repeat herself and both of their frustrations continued until my father laughed and said, "Melanie, I can't remember. Tell me now and then let's go over it in three months! I'll remember then." My sister burst into laughter. My father's joke about the loss of short-term memory before long-term memory has been repeated many times within our family and it never gets old. This reaction is more a reflection of my father's pure heart that he strives to preserve in the light of divine providence.

Faith laughs along with my father and family. It helps us realize that the height of holiness is reached through what we are already doing and enduring in life, because everything we count as trivial and worthless is what can actually make us holy.

THE VIRTUE OF HONESTY

Being a man of authority, my father has always been able to recognize strength and weaknesses in his subordinates. He also applied that same discernment to himself. Since he had a healthy view of his own strengths and weaknesses, he would purposely surround himself with others who could complement them. This sobriety of opinion and authentic meekness has won my father the praise and esteem of many people in diverse fields. And this personal honesty was apparent when he turned to my older brother and confessed, "A.J., I don't think I should drive anymore." He knew that he was missing turns, not seeing street signs, and could no longer adequately judge the distance between his vehicle and pedestrians.

When my brother told me the story, I was moved by the integrity of my father's decision. I could not imagine the depth of surrender to divine providence that led him to realize and accept that driving a vehicle was no longer "his part" in the plan of life. Giving up driving in the Western world is surrendering independence—we lose a huge degree of control over our own lives. In giving up his ability to drive, my father not only accepted reality, but he also gave his children a tender gift of charity. My father preserved us from any heartbreaking conversation that would have forced us kids to take away his keys.

With my father's typical jovial wit, when I asked him about how he felt with not being able to drive anymore, he joked and said, "Well, I've been driving your mother around for most of our lives. I figured it was her turn!"

Faith hails such acts of surrender. It teaches us that we must put all speculation aside and, with childlike willingness, accept all that God presents to us. What God arranges for us to experience at each moment is the best and holiest thing that could happen to us.

THE VIRTUE OF GENTLENESS

As my father's disease runs its course, he continues to easily surrender to divine providence. While our family continues to struggle with questions of why, he has found the answer in God's care and is at peace. And in this peace he receives joy and is able to laugh. No matter the situation, he meets it head-on with grace and humor.

Recently my father's weight loss concerned my mother, so she took him to the doctors. The doctor asked him, "What's going on? Are you eating?" "Yes," he replied. "Do you have any abdominal pain?" "No," he replied. "Well, why are you losing weight?" My father, with the peace that comes from trusting

God, explained, "Well, Doctor, I go to get something and forget. Then I walk back and forget. Then I go back and forget again. And then I walk back to where I was and then walk to get what I needed. I'm just doing a lot of walking!" Needless to say, this had everyone laughing. This is the joy and lightheartedness of a soul that has been surrendered and consecrated to God and is truly at rest in his divine providence.

Faith chuckles at my father's joke. It explains that God reveals himself to the humble in the lowliest of disguises, but the proud, who never look below the surface, fail to find him even in his greatest manifestations. This is the witness of my father to divine providence.

OUR SURRENDER

Honestly, I had great reservations about sharing my father's story with you. It is a personal narrative that is still being written and that still carries a lot of pain. My father's witness, however, is not only for me or my family. It is a witness for all of us struggling to see God's goodness and surrender to his divine providence. It is one person's experience, in the context of his life, of how the good and the bad, the ugly and the beautiful, have been approached, received, and baptized in the light of divine providence. It is a testimony to each of us of the vast array of virtues that are born within us when we accept divine providence. In this acceptance, we can find hope, redemptive suffering, peace, a sense of humor, and whatever other virtues we might need—or that those around us might need.

In light of this witness, I would like to invite us all to dive more deeply into a holistic abandonment to divine providence. We can begin to ask, "What is my part in the work of divine providence? How can I do it well and responsibly? How can I nurture the virtues of a good life by my surrender to the presence and ways of God?"

SPIRITUAL STEPS

Some practical thoughts to help us all live the wisdom of divine providence:

- What virtue most helps you see God's presence? Thank God for that virtue and your ability to see him through it.
- What virtue do you most struggle to live? How does God want to reveal himself to you through it? How can this awareness help you better fight for this virtue in your life?
- Stop and track how one virtue networks other virtues. Recognize how God's beauty and care for us can be seen through them.
- Name people who have exemplified certain virtues and how these virtues have reflected God's presence and graciousness to our world today.

CLOSING PRAYER

All-holy and loving God,
you are my beginning and end.
Show me your goodness.
Guide me to live in your grace
and to dwell in your divine warmth.
Help me to live your way of love and to walk along
your path of mercy.
Lord, be with me. Strengthen me.
Let my virtues and those of my neighbors
show me your presence.
Help me to always dwell in your providence.
I make this prayer through Jesus Christ,
who is Lord, forever and ever.
Amen.

Complete Surrender to the Will of God Is the Essence of Spirituality

OPENING INVITATION

- Set aside your worries of the day.
- Take some deep breaths. Invite God into your day.
- Ask God to speak to you through this day's wisdom.
- Begin when you are ready!

THE INTENTION OF OUR BLESSED AUTHOR

Fr. Caussade makes the bold declaration that God has compelled him to share this message of divine providence as a help to those who seek to be holy and are discouraged. He identifies himself as a spiritual guide with answers to our questions. He seeks to calm the storm of our lives, slow its pace, and speak words of wisdom and comfort to each of us. He gently requests, "So do please try and learn from me."

As we dive into the vast treasury and beauty of his masterpiece, Fr. Caussade gives us a smile, a pat on the back, or a nudge, and points our hearts to the sure path of abandonment to divine providence. He emphasizes the vital role of the spiritual life. He compares its functions to those of our bodies, without which we would die in this life. The comparison is clear. If our bodies die without their necessities, so our souls will harden and die without their necessities. Fr. Caussade asks what could be more vital than breathing, eating, and sleeping? And what is easier? He applies this awareness to the spiritual life and teaches us that love and loyalty are just as vital and so they cannot be as difficult to acquire as we imagine. Yes, that latter part shows that while our blessed author is firm, he is also very encouraging. He tells us that the path to spiritual maturity and holiness is not insurmountable. It can be done.

In the message of divine providence, there are no ifs, ands, or buts. There is only the present moment, the call from God, and the sure and easy path to holiness. It is a holiness that can be received by all people, in any place, and in the midst of any struggle.

Do we comprehend what this path to holiness truly involves? Do we grasp our call to be holy? Are we working on it?

Divine providence has no time for negligence and gives no excuse for any dismissiveness toward the universal call to holiness. Holiness is found right here and now. Holiness is looking for God's presence where we are and not where we would prefer to be. It is seeing God's goodness in circumstances or people we would rather not. Holiness is leaving the world of fantasy and wishful thinking and being in the present moment. It is being attentive to where we are and doing what we are doing. Not existing in the future, not despairing over our lives by comparing them to others, but accepting God's providence that is at our fingertips.

Holiness, therefore, can be nurtured in the ordinary and mundane things of life, in the duties and responsibilities of our vocation, and in the attentive fulfillment of the moral law and precepts of the Church. Divine providence expects nothing less. It directs us with fatherly kindness to live this life of abandonment in every situation and in every responsibility of our lives. It convicts us to do our part and leave the rest to God. In giving this yes to God, faith shows us how we can receive every grace and virtue we need in order to do our part well and grow in holiness.

This summons can be abrupt at times. It has no sympathy for empty intellectualism. It mocks those who know theological truths brilliantly, teaches them to others and gives spiritual advice about them, but do not themselves have any experience of these truths. Faith tells us that such people will be compared to those who actually do God's will, even without deep academic knowledge. Such scholars are like doctors who are ill, while those without medical training enjoy perfect health.

Divine providence escalates the call and shows us that holiness is produced by God's will and our acceptance of it. It is not produced by intellectual speculation about it.

We see in this criticism a strong focus on the practical aspects of life. Faith calls us to ask questions and try to know and follow God's will in the midst of joys and sorrows.

Spiritual wisdom shows us that people who are trying to be holy would be saved a lot of trouble if they were taught to virtuously live and find God in the ordinary aspects of their lives.

With a kind heart, therefore, we are all invited to realize that the demands of holiness are nothing extraordinary. We just need to carry on as we are doing, and to endure what we have to do, but with a changed attitude. And this change is simply to say "I will" to all that God asks of us.

THE HOLY FAMILY

Of all the places that divine providence could take us, it should not surprise us that it leads us to the example of the Holy Family of Jesus, Mary, and Joseph. The call to holiness takes us right into the intimacy and simplicity of this preeminent family and highlights how the Holy Family did their part and left the rest to God.

In particular, we highlight the person of Mary. She is the embodiment of all the mystical theology of our Old Testament ancestors. She is a figure of Israel who is endowed with divine promises and prophecies, and the best summation of the entire human family's hunger for God and his righteousness. Divine wisdom lifts the veil of false deference and teaches us how to ask the poignant question: What made Mary so singular in her devotion?

Faith does not leave us hanging. It answers our question. Mary was the simplest of humans and the one who made the most complete surrender of herself to God. This frame of mind was the foundation of Mary's entire spiritual life. And so Mary's power did not come from herself. It came from her complete abandonment to God's providence, and this abandonment filled her with every grace and virtue she needed in her life.

Fr. Caussade expands our understanding of Mary's surrender by powerfully combining and comparing her declaration: "Let it be with me according to your word" (Lk 1:38) with the words of her divine Son, "Your will be done." These words were first given by the Lord Jesus in his instruction on prayer (see Matthew 6:10) but were later repeated by him in the midst of his Passion in the garden of Gethsemane (see Matthew 26:42). In merging the words of Mary with these heartfelt and blood-stained words of the Lord Jesus, Fr. Caussade is showing us how essential Mary's abandonment is in her life and in God's plan of salvation. He explains that magnificent events certainly occurred in Mary's life but her frame of mind was always one of surrender, and it included each and every area of her life. All of her actions were needed for God to give his blessings. Fr. Caussade teaches us that no matter what her jobs were—ordinary, commonplace, or seemingly more important ones—they all revealed to her—sometimes quite clearly, sometimes obscure-ly—the activity of the Almighty. They were all a constant oppor-tunity for her to see and adore God.

This truth cannot be underestimated. Every part of Mary's life, from washing laundry to cleaning her house, was a part of her surrender to divine providence. Yes, each of these tasks was a part of God's plan and a means for her to serve and praise him. Mary was filled with joy and regarded everything she had to do or suffer at any moment of her life as a gift from God.

Earlier in his teachings, Fr. Caussade expresses this joy himself and takes a somewhat comical view of the archangel Gabriel's visit to Mary. While certainly sharing in the glory of the annunciation, our spiritual master is quick to point out, "The angel had his moment." It was one awesome moment, but for this time-shattering event to have happened, and for it to have lasting power, Mary had to surrender every day and in every way to the providence of God. The same providence that sent her Gabriel is the same providence that asked her to cook supper, sweep the floor, or go to the well for water.

All the events of Mary's life, and our own, must be seen as beautiful, holistic narratives, and each moment offers its own grace and peace.

Our task, then, is to accept God's grace and discern his pres-ence and purpose in all that we do. We have to imitate Mary and not be deceived by the commonality, repetition, or mundane nature of the tasks of life. God is with us. We have to enlighten the shadows and find his presence in all that we do so that we can live the virtues needed in the present moment.

Of course, Mary was not alone. She was the mother of the God-Man and the wife of Joseph. She lived in a family and managed a home. In particular, Mary and Joseph worked hard and undertook many duties and tasks so as to earn their *daily bread*. Fr. Caussade uses actual material bread as a symbol for God's providence and asks us to ponder what the real bread was that nourished the faith of Mary and Joseph.

The question should not sit. Divine providence gives us a robust answer in showing us the sacrament of the moment. Using the symbol of bread, we can see how the Holy Family lived in the presence of God through their daily labor. As a sacrament is defined as a visible sign of invisible grace, so every moment can be a kind of sacrament. The visible task that we are undertaking can become a means for us to encounter God, receive his grace, and live according to his will. Everything we do can be an avenue to meet God and grow in virtue.

Faith is going to great lengths to reveal to us the presence and power of God in our lives. It is inviting us to do our part, to see God in the present moment and in our daily tasks, so that we can trust him and abandon ourselves to the goodness and comfort of his divine providence.

PEACE IN THE PRESENT MOMENT

Using the Holy Family as an example, we have a description of the central tenets of surrendering to divine providence. These tenets include: drawing close to God, cooperating with his will, living in the present moment, fulfilling the duties of our lives, and finding God's peace in this world.

Faith regularly encourages us to surrender to divine providence and make our surrender tangible by a virtuous and prayerful life. Faith reveals to us that the path of surrendering to the ways of God is obvious. It is right in front of us, and it does not require anything outrageous. It is offered to us all the time, wherever we are. It flows through every fiber of our body and soul until it reaches the very core of our being.

In emphasizing the proximity of holiness, divine wisdom shows us *cooperation* with God. The word is best understood as being a partner (*co-*) in the workings of God, namely, in his "operations." And so to cooperate is a central aspect of surrendering to divine providence. The designs of God—what he chooses to do; his will, his actions, and his grace—are all one and the same thing, all working together to enable us to reach perfection. This perfection is neither more nor less than our faithful cooperation with God. We have to welcome and engage God's presence and grace in our daily lives.

In cooperating with divine providence, the world of grace is opened to us and we receive the pressing invitation to intentionally undertake the duties and responsibilities of our lives with a deeper understanding of God's presence and purpose in all things. Divine providence teaches us that all our moments are made productive by our obedience to the will of God, which reveals itself in a thousand different ways, each of which successively becomes our immediate duty. God's will is all-wise and all-powerful. It is infinitely kind to all who trust it completely and without reserve and who do not go around seeking other, lesser, or disordered things.

Faith seeks to lead us as it announces, "Accept what is before you and then do your part in his plan!" It is the reality at hand that is more spiritually profitable for us than any number of other aspirations or hopes for a later or different time. We are challenged to see the arrangements of divine providence here and now. All things owe their nature, reality, and strength to the will of God, which arranges them all so that they can benefit our souls. Yes! This is the heart of the teaching on divine providence. We cannot fully comprehend the infinity of God's plan, and so we should trust. *God has so arranged all things so that the present moment is our best moment.*

The present moment, the here and now—wherever that might be—is the best opportunity for us to do our part in our pursuit of holiness. This is the essence of our abandonment to divine providence. It is accepting that we are not called to be somewhere else or to do something else. *We are called to be right here and right now!* This is where God wants us, where he seeks to meet us, and he has moved heaven and earth for us to be at this appointed time and place with him. It does not matter what ideas fill our minds or what our bodies feel; whether our minds are distracted and worried or our bodies are suffering and dying. The will of God is always in the present moment and is the very life of the body and soul no matter what condition they are in. We are sustained—soul and body—by God's will alone.

In featuring the sacredness of the present moment, faith presents the duties of our lives in a very positive and sanctifying way. Our everyday duties and commitments are the ordinary means to holiness. We are summoned to embrace these tasks, perform them virtuously, and find God in the midst of them. We are fed, strengthened, purified, enriched, and made holy through the faithful fulfillment of our duties in the present moment.

Faith nudges us. It underlines the basic truth of our duties by asking the stark question, "Do we think that we can find peace by resisting God?" Faith is unceasing as it shows us what resistance to God is all about, how we double down in this opposition, and why it is the source of all our trouble. By neglecting or rebelling against God in the present moment, it is only fitting that we should not find contentment in anything else.

In developing the process of doing our part and abandoning ourselves to divine providence, we can find internal peace. Such an unsurpassable peace is the rich fruit of an abandonment to God. This peace confirms within us that there is nothing more beneficial to us than God's will, and there is absolutely nothing that gives us more peace or does more to make us holy than obeying God's will.

The process of abandonment to divine providence is both demanding and consoling. It is gentle yet firm toward us; one movement leading us to the other so that each of us knows how to abandon ourselves and dwell within God's abundant providence. And so we see how tangible and accessible holiness is and how we are all invited to cooperate with God. From these movements we are shown the sacrament of the present moment and the importance of our duties. By doing our part, fulfilling these duties, and seeing God's presence in all things, we are presented with the peace that is tenderly offered to us by God in his infinite kindness.

Will we accept the invitation to surrender to divine providence? Will we search for God's presence in our lives and live the virtues flowing from it? Will we focus on the peace that God offers us and do our part to receive it? The invitation is given, the search must begin, God's peace awaits us!

SPIRITUAL STEPS

Some practical thoughts to help us all live the wisdom of divine providence:

- Discern the schedule of your day and its activities. Where do you look for consolation? Is it with a cup of coffee, in a friend's smile, during time on social media, and so on?
- In these moments, are you trying to find God's consolation and peace without God? Ask yourself, "Is this a part of my surrender to God or a break from it?"

- Obsessive activity usually indicates a break from surrender. Good things are worth enjoying in moderation. Ask yourself, "What activities have become small acts of rebellion against my surrender to God's providence?"
- Resolve ways in which to temper activities that have become obsessive. Seek to broaden your life and to find God in other activities, especially those within your duties in life.

CLOSING PRAYER

Almighty and eternal God,
you are all-good, and you call me to yourself.
Let me not be distracted.
Show me your presence. Help me to find you
throughout my day.
Lord, be with me. Guide me.
In the things I do well, let me rejoice in you.
In the things I struggle with, let me rely on you.
Help me to always dwell in your providence.
I make this prayer through Jesus Christ,
who is Lord, forever and ever.
Amen.

Only Complete and True Faith Enables the Soul to Accept with Joy Everything That Happens to It

OPENING INVITATION

- Set aside your worries of the day.
- Take some deep breaths. Invite God into your day.
- Ask God to speak to you through this day's wisdom.
- Begin when you are ready!

GOD'S PRESENCE IN THE DARKNESS

We need to understand the twists and turns of God's providence as we go through the throes of life. In particular, we need to realize the challenge of truly abandoning ourselves to the will and ways of God.

After receiving a beautiful panorama of the way of abandonment, we now enter into a more mysterious part of the spiritual life. The tone and demeanor change. We now encounter a more mystical part of divine providence. In these teachings, we not only draw from Fr. Caussade's Jesuit spirituality but also from the spiritual treasury of Sts. John of the Cross and Teresa of Avila of the Carmelite Order. We will draw from this treasury in order to describe the darkness that can sometimes accompany our journey with God.

Yes, the darkness—it can bewilder even the greatest of believers. And so let's explore this sense of nothingness and how Fr. Caussade and other spiritual writers explain it.

AN INITIAL MOVE TOWARD GOD

In life, believers can follow moral laws and Church rules without ever fully following God with all their mind, heart, and strength. They are simply what Fr. Caussade calls "average Christians," and he wants more for them and for us. He explains that in the journey with God, we will periodically be given moments of conversion. These are turnaround opportunities when we can say yes to God and begin to see and encounter him more clearly and know of his presence more intimately in our lives. These moments often happen when God gives us a tragedy, crisis, or a pressing sense of being lost. Such experiences can happen quietly, as with a laborer working at his job or a student studying at her desk, or very dramatically, as with a father being diagnosed with dementia or a corporate professional unexpectedly losing her job.

If we try to live in the present moment, then God will allow more of these sacred encounters in our lives. If we accept these times of conversion, then God will take us deeper into the mysteries of his life. As this happens, we are called to live out more radically our abandonment to his divine providence. This will happen in what the Carmelite tradition calls the "purgative way." While Fr. Caussade does not use this specific term, he is certainly speaking about the same reality and its transformative power in our hearts.

The purgative way is the way of the beginner in the spiritual life. It is when the average Christian realizes that there is more to a life of faith and begins to desire it. During the purgative way, we are called to abandon a life according to the flesh, which only sees things in materialistic or utilitarian ways, and seek to walk more closely in God's presence.

THE PURGATIVE WAY

In the purgative way, our souls undergo a serious purification. Our hearts are ordered to God and his path of goodness and love. God's grace brings about a process of spiritual refinement, healing, and a reconstitution of who we are in God's eyes and under his protective care. The purgative way, however, actually has two principal phases. First, there is a time of consolation and then, second, a time of darkness and desolation. These phases can be a cycle within our souls, depending on our openness to God's activity. If we backslide, then the initial process has to be repeated. If we are faithful, the process occurs again so as to take us even deeper into spiritual realities and the presence of God in our lives.

After a moment of conversion, the purgative way begins with graces of consolation. During this initial phase, we emotionally feel God's presence. Our hearts are overjoyed, and his presence is uplifting. We enjoy praying, and it can be accompanied by moments of euphoria. We see the effects of our prayer, and everything seems crystal-clear and edifying. Since the soul is just starting on the path of the spiritual life, God is giving these comforts and indulgences so as to reveal to us the delicacies of his presence and the joys of his divine will.

After our soul has been so pampered, however, God leads us to the next phase of the purgative way, which is cathartic. Suddenly our emotions go numb; we cannot feel God's presence, and our euphoria is replaced by a sense of sorrow. We are not sure where God has gone or if we have done something wrong. It seems our prayers go unanswered, and we are not sure if God is listening. We feel isolated, alone, and deserted.

We need to realize why this is happening to us. This is not a moral darkness or a darkness of divine disfavor. As the graces of consolation are suspended, God is actually giving us different graces in order for us to be closer to him. God is showering us with subtle graces of obedience, which is a word that comes from Latin and means "to listen." Our soul is now called to persevere through a purification that allows it to hear God and worship God as himself and not for what he can do for us. We are led to adore the all-powerful God of consolation *rather than the passing consolations of God*. In this darkness of the purgative way, God brings order to our soul and leads it to spiritual maturity.

While we may not feel it, God is closer to us and is able to bring about a greater work within us in this time of darkness than in the time of previous consolation. It is very important that we realize how normal this uncomfortable darkness is in the search to be with God and abandon ourselves to his divine providence.

God is showing us the depth of his presence precisely by suspending our emotional experience. We are being taught to encounter God with or without emotional satisfaction, with or without perceivable results, and with or without getting what we want when we want it. During the purgative way, God is calling us to mature. He is unveiling to us the infinite horizon of his divine providence. In this revelation he is also healing our old wounds, lessening our ego, elevating our spirit, exposing our inordinate self-love, and naming and banishing moral faults and weaknesses from within us. In this purgation, God is disclosing to us the waywardness of sin and its hurtful consequences to our relationship with him, our neighbors, and our world.

In the purgative way, we wrestle to trust God and abandon ourselves to the goodness of his divine providence. In laboring for this abandonment, we begin to yearn for virtue, the elevation of spiritual freedom, and the joy of being with God.

As we seek these spiritual riches, we understand and want to be purged from all obvious and sensual sins. We want to denounce any base desires that take us away from God's presence and goodness. God lets us fully experience our own weakness as we try to solve our own essential dilemma: we are fallen and cannot help ourselves. This is the most basic and principal admission of the purgative way. We cannot change ourselves. We need God's help. In this experience we see the depth and purpose of the purgative way. We see our own sinfulness and helplessness, and we come to a fuller knowledge of how wonderful and attractive God's providence is and how much we want to surrender to it and be a part of it.

As God works in our souls during the purgative way, we are called to know of his presence and his work to bring about a new identity within us. This is not easy or comfortable. The process of spiritual regeneration can be a time of great anxiety and restlessness. Our minds are being enlightened, our memories are being enriched, our imaginations are being elevated, and our wills are being strengthened. Our emotions can be uncertain and a cross for us in the purgative way. They will especially need to be matured by grace so that our capacity for love can be increased. The purgative way, therefore, is a time of self-sacrifice and vigilance so that we can abandon ourselves to divine providence, God's work can be done, and we can see ourselves more gloriously in his providential light.

THE GRACES OF CONVERSION

Early in my priesthood, a middle-aged woman, whom I will call June, joined the parish RCIA program. June felt a strong call to draw closer to God. She was raised Catholic, and so she returned to her roots and asked for help. June was directed to the RCIA and soon entered the yearlong process of Christian formation. In the course of the year, she flourished in her relationship with God. In one RCIA class, the word *conversion* was explained. The word was defined in its proper depth. Rather than meaning a simple transfer from one religion to another, conversion actually indicates an intensification in one's surrender to God.

June later explained to me that this clarification was life-changing for her. She began to see a larger picture, and this led her to discern the splendor and beauty of God's providence. This awareness led her to begin a regular prayer life. At first, June received various spiritual consolations and healings, but then she hit a wall. She did not understand why things suddenly became so arid and seemingly lifeless. June was guided in the basic tenets of the purgative way and she persevered. She did not like the confusion and uncertainty. She did not know why God was hiding from her and why her spiritual life resembled, in her words, "a game of peekaboo." June trusted in God. She fought on and God blessed her with new illuminations.

June accepted the ways of divine providence. She still had unanswered questions. Well, that is until her father called and told her about his cancer. June was very close to him, and she took it very hard. Thanks be to God, she was able to retire early and take care of the older man. There were numerous medical tests, agonizing waiting periods for results, more tests, treatment options, and medication upon medication. It would have been too much for most people, but June rocked it. She surprised even herself at how smoothly she took things, the joy she found in her heart, and the patience she showed in the face of her father's frustration with the medical staff, pharmacists, home health nurses, and the army of other people involved in her father's care.

Only after the older man was cleared and in remission was June able to reflect clearly on the whole experience. In a conversation with her, she shared with me, "Father, now I understand the purgative way. It was not a game, it was all a preparation." Amazingly, June made the connection between the selflessness and virtue that was nurtured in her during the purgative way with the peace, joy, and patience she was able to preserve while caring for her father. This was action born from contemplation! This is the consistency found in people who have abandoned themselves to divine providence. It is the joy of those who know of God's loving-kindness and care for us no matter what happens.

This is the way of life offered to us all. This is the joy to which we are all invited. In order to accept this way and receive this joy, we simply have to abandon ourselves to God's providence and trust in his goodness. This is our standing invitation. What will we do with it?

A NEW PEOPLE

Fr. Caussade acknowledges that people who live lives of abandonment to divine providence will be anomalies. Many people, even average Christians, will not understand them and will openly mock them. They will consider such people to be so heavenly minded that they're worth no earthly good. Fr. Caussade points out, however, that such people ridicule what they do not understand. As people who have not entered into the realm of divine providence, they have no context or true comprehension of God's benevolence and the legitimacy of an unconditional trust in him.

Our esteemed author teaches us that such misunderstanding and persecution are also part of the purgative way. Such rejection should be welcomed and received with humility and compassion. We are called to embrace the way of abandonment, ignore the opinions of others, and live joyfully in the embrace of God's providence.

A WIDOW'S TESTIMONY OF JOY

As we explore the depth of the teachings on spiritual darkness and surrendering to divine providence, it would be helpful to look at an unexpected example of such a surrender and the joy that comes with it.

Some time ago, I was making pastoral visits to various homebound parishioners. One such visit was to a parishioner who celebrated a major birthday milestone. She warmly greeted me and welcomed me into her home. She was surrounded by children, grandchildren, and a few great-grandchildren. She was truly a beloved matriarch. As we sat together, I asked all the usual questions of someone with such age and wisdom, but unlike others, she had some funny and entertaining answers. The litany that summarized her answers, and the account of her earlier life with her late husband, was simply, "Oh, Father, there was so much joy." And her life reflected that joy.

As our conversation came to a close, she offered some unsolicited but greatly appreciated counsel. She asked me, "Father, do you know what the secret was of our joy?" I nodded and asked, "What was it?" She smiled, leaned back, and told me, "God was always first." The message was strong enough, especially as she lifted her pointer finger heavenward as she gave her answer. But the holy widow was not done. She continued, "God was always first, and that started with a tithe. Yes, even with eight children, we always gave our first 10 percent to God. It wasn't easy, but it always reminded us that God is first. You know, Father, you can't trust money. But you can always trust God."

I was speechless. The testimony of "God first" was amazing enough, but the radical credibility of a consistent tithe was inspiring. Our visit was coming to an end but she repeated herself and told me, "We showed up for God, and he always showed up for us. Sometimes he made us wait, but he always came through." She laughed, and it was a laugh that indicated a mature knowledge of God's purgative way. It was clear that memories were going through her mind as she kept a gentle smile on her face.

The testimony of this holy widow, much like the widow praised by the Lord Jesus in the Gospel for offering her two mites (see Mark 12:41–44) is a practical example of the secret of joy, namely, the secret of always putting God first. Even when things are uncertain and God is purifying us, we know that he is with us. He is first. And joy is the reward of a life surrendered to his divine providence. It is a gift that is widely received by souls that have accepted the gentle yoke of God's providence.

In our lives, we are invited to make this same surrender and experience this same joy. Will we? In the throes of life, along with all its joys and sorrows, will we also turn and accept God's providence and care for us and our world?

SPIRITUAL STEPS

Some practical thoughts to help us all live the wisdom of divine providence:

- Identify times in your life when a time of darkness brought about an unexpected good.

- Purposely choose times in your day to pray when you would otherwise not pray. Ask yourself if prayer at that time brought additional graces or insights.
- In moments of darkness, recall times of great joy and consolation. Ask God what good he seeks to bring to you or to others through your darkness.
- Look for others who might be in moments of darkness and speak words of encouragement to them.

CLOSING PRAYER

God of all radiance,
you are the path of goodness
and the source of every illumination.
Pour your grace into me.
Let me know your will and help me
to relish in your presence.
In times of darkness, help me hold on to you.
In moments of uncertainty, let me cling to you.
In areas of confusion, let me embrace you.
In all things, Lord, let me surrender
to your divine providence.
Be my light and my strength.
Guide me in your will and bless me with your joy.
Help me to always dwell in your providence.
I make this prayer through Jesus Christ,
who is Lord, forever and ever.
Amen.

All Will Be Well If We Abandon Ourselves to God

OPENING INVITATION

- Set aside your worries of the day.
- Take some deep breaths. Invite God into your day.
- Ask God to speak to you through this day's wisdom.
- Begin when you are ready!

NO BYSTANDERS

After learning about the teachings on the abandonment to divine providence, we must now turn our attention to the active work that we are called to in the world. Truly we can say "It's time to get to work!" Rather than taking the posture of a bystander or thinking that we have no role in the workings of divine providence, we are led to action. It is an action born from contemplation. It is as if the saintly priest is rallying us and calling out to us, "There is evil in the world, abandon yourself to divine providence, and now go and fight for goodness!"

While not enjoyable for its own sake, the willingness to stand up and even suffer persecution for the sake of goodness can be an opportunity for conversion in us and witness to the world around us. Our example exposes injustice, evil, and offense. Evil has a way of perpetuating a false narrative about its inevitability and seeks to convince us that we are victims and have no power to stop or battle against forces of wickedness. Our ability to be a "sign of contradiction" and a voice of reason and moral truth serves to wake up others, show them the encroaching darkness, and lead them to struggle against it.

Moral darkness and evil rely on silence, isolation, and fear in order to shame the one who stands for truth and goodness. As we grow spiritually and see God's providence in our world, we are less drawn by the allure of vanity and the desire for human respect. We become stronger and feel compelled to name evil, promote what is good, and defend what is beautiful and innocent. This willingness edifies us and expands our ability to see divine providence and hunger and thirst for righteousness.

Our world is fallen and our race is sinful, and so when difficulty comes because of our stance for goodness, we are prepared for suffering and persecution. We graciously accept them not as a blessing in themselves but as a means of sharing God's grace with all men and women. Such acceptance on our part of whatever divine providence permits can mold and shape us into better people who are even more receptive and reliant on divine providence. As we see God's providence and become active participants in it, we experience its transformative power and quiet force of goodness working in and through us. This makes divine providence irresistible as we tangibly sense its reality and practically discern its authority. It all becomes very real to us and we grasp how imminent goodness can be if we keep saying yes.

In this growing awareness, it is as if scales fall from our eyes and we begin to recognize the palpable nature of divine providence and our capacity to be its instrument in our world. We realize, "Evil happens, but I can champion goodness. Evil only wins if I do nothing." The false sense of powerlessness is unmasked. The facade falls and grace flows. Our invitation is to enter and work within this tide of grace.

As our hearts deepen in their surrender to divine providence, we come to realize more profoundly that we each have unique gifts and talents that have been given to us for a reason and with a mission by divine providence. We comprehend these abilities anew and perceive them as gifts by which we can spread kindness, peace, and compassion in our world.

THE SOURCE OF EVIL

As a Christian, Fr. Caussade knew and taught the truths given by the Christian tradition. Among these truths was the biblical explanation of the source of evil. This teaching is a necessary panorama for us to fully understand the summons to fight for goodness. And so here is a summary of this teaching and why it is important.

The Christian faith sees suffering and evil as the tragic consequence of the original sin of humanity's first parents. Adam and Eve disobeyed and seized a majesty above the natural human state. God's love for us, however, was shown in the aftermath of this disobedience. Rather than vengeance, God searched out his wayward children and showed his care. It was a concern that was kind but also one that called for them to receive the consequences of their actions. And so the original sin of our first parents caused the Fall—ours and all of creation's—from God's grace. It was a disaster with lasting effects. The Fall broke the peace between God and humanity, within our bodies and souls, within the human community, and between us and the rest of creation.

On account of the Fall, God is now feared. Caricatures are invented of him that present him as an angry and vengeful deity. Rather than seeing God as our loving Father, our fallenness turns him into a monster that seeks to hurt or destroy us. How can we surrender to divine providence if this is our view of God?

Original sin also weakened our human nature. Our intellects are now clouded and distracted, our wills are wounded and inclined to evil, our memories and imaginations are distracted and wayward, and our emotions are immature and impulsive. Overall, our souls are now in a fragile state and our bodies are corruptible. We are caught in a tension between the desires of the body and those of the spirit. We find a battle within ourselves for goodness as we are created good but inclined to darkness.

Original sin also diminished our relationship with our neighbors. In particular, now there is tension between spouses in marriage, which then spreads to families, workplaces, friends, and society as a whole. We no longer are naturally inclined to humility, kindness, and selfless service. We see self-pity, resentment, anger, jealousy, and selfishness within relationships and in our own hearts. Peace is in jeopardy. Life is marked by a restlessness and a desire for power and control. How can we live well in a community and be an instrument of divine providence when our neighbors are seen as competitors rather than brothers and sisters?

Original sin also caused friction between the human family and the rest of creation. We approach the world as a tyrant rather than a steward. Instead of approaching the world with prudence and temperance, we cause it irreparable harm for reasons of profit and domination. How can we live in peace when we destroy our natural home?

All the inclinations above are causes of the Fall and they bring about nothing but chaos and evil. For these to be healed, elevated, and reordered, we need grace. Grace gives us freedom and allows peace to be restored. But what about freedom?

The moral law instructs us on what is right and what is wrong. It shows us our sinfulness as would a demanding tutor, admonishing and correcting us. As we open ourselves and allow moral truth to teach us, it prepares our hearts for freedom. This truth regularly calls us to fulfill the moral law and our duties according to our state in life. Freedom is often falsely defined as an ability to do whatever we want. If this is true, how can grace work? How can we accept divine providence if everything, even moral goodness, revolves solely around us and our own specific desires and passions? No, freedom is not the ability to do whatever we want. Such a definition is more akin to barbarism. Real freedom is the power to do what is right. It is the capacity to discern and surrender to divine providence and live according to it. If we are left to our own inclinations then we are not free because, in our fallenness, we will very quickly become slaves to our own sinful passions and pride.

In being formed well by the moral law, freedom is an openness to divine providence. It seeks to discover God's will in each situation and in every moment. As we respond and nurture freedom, we grow in spiritual maturity as we are empowered to act above our passions and desires. We begin to recognize God's presence among us and recognize his divine providence. We develop an unexplainable attraction to its beauty and internal order, and we begin to desire that same harmony in our own lives.

For this to grow, we have to cooperate with God's grace and seek to live a life of discipline, selflessness, and goodness. But this is not easy. Divine providence knows this struggle and yet God believes in us and calls us to such a life.

THE EXAMPLE OF TOTAL ABANDONMENT

Being all-knowing, all-loving, and all-powerful, God offers us a new beginning in Jesus Christ. By his Cross and Resurrection, Jesus Christ destroys sin, heals its disorder, reestablishes tranquility, secures our freedom, and offers us peace. He laid down his life as an ambassador of this message and the hope it brings to humanity. The cause of evil and moral darkness is real but the power of God's grace shines forth from the Resurrection. He knew of its capacity to bring about harmony and goodness. It is exactly this faith that enlivens our call to surrender to divine providence and that lets grace work within us and through us.

The eternal Son of God comes to each of us and offers us salvation. He lived a fully human life, and by his saving mission brought about reconciliation between our fallen race and God the Father. Therefore, in the person of Jesus Christ we see the possibility of a new beginning of peace for the human family, marked by a tranquility of order between God and humanity, within our own hearts, among our neighbors, and between humanity and the rest of creation. In Jesus Christ, we are offered this peace. It is a peace that requires our cooperation with grace, which is the life of God within us. For those who seek and are willing to fight for goodness, grace is offered and can be effective in bringing about a restored peace.

In taking on our human nature, the Lord Jesus embraced our suffering, body and soul. He chose to accept and use suffering as the very means by which he would surrender to divine providence and show us God's plan of redemption from evil and sin. Jesus took upon himself all the sins of humanity throughout time. He bore the totality of human guilt and alienation.

FR. CAUSSADE'S CALL

While the saving ministry of Jesus Christ destroyed sin and its darkness, the consequences of sin still remain in our world. But suffering can now become a source of righteousness, and grace helps us bring goodness and peace to our world. Fr. Caussade is not perpetuating empty optimism or wishful thinking when he calls us to go out and fight for goodness. He knows the real power of grace and wants us to cooperate with it, so that righteousness can vanquish sin and light can dispel darkness.

As a Christian and a spiritual master, Fr. Caussade knew the power of God's grace and the mission given to us by a God, who magnificently dwells in the present moment and who constantly seeks what is best for us. We are exhorted to live a life that reflects this act of surrender. We must understand the mission and generously respond to it for the sake of all that is good in our world.

In light of this mission, some popular fears are turned upside down. In a life committed to divine providence, we no longer fear our enemies, we are not compelled to justify ourselves, and we receive everything back in a better manner than how we first offered it to God. In the end, a life abandoned to divine providence can be beneficial and transformative for us and for those around us. We are called to pick up the mantle, throw back evil, and work for a civilization of love.

Each of us according to our own state in life is called to speak truth, fight for goodness, and share beauty. Such a path is not easy nor comfortable, but it is worth the struggle as grace brings light, hope, and a righteousness of life that gives us abundant joy.

As God's passive will allows for evil to be done, so his grace is ready to counter it. We just have to be willing to surrender to divine providence and be the instruments of that grace in our world today.

Will we? Will we respond to the pressing call given by this spiritual master? Will we choose to make a difference for the sake of goodness?

A BROTHER'S WITNESS

I started our journey through the spiritual writing of Fr. Caussade with the story of my father and his acceptance of divine providence through his diagnosis of dementia. As any family knows, when one member is suffering, every member shares in it. In order for the suffering and its darkness to be placed in its proper context and not become absolutized, where it is the end all and be all of a person and a family, the counsel and call of Fr. Caussade must be heeded. Each family member must rally goodness and stir virtue. For the sorrow not to take over, the family must carry and share light and joy. This has been the lesson of Fr. Caussade for us in this final chapter of his masterpiece.

This summons within my own family was particularly picked up by my older brother. Like my father, he served in the army. He distinguished himself in the 82nd Airborne, and later in his military career he received a Bronze Star for meritorious action while in Afghanistan. He is the firstborn, whom we jokingly call Number One in the family, and he and my father have always been close. My brother bears my father's name, Alan Joseph, and so we have always just called him A.J. My parents started their family young and, in many respects, my brother and parents grew up together.

Shortly after my father's diagnosis, my brother retired from the military. He was in his mid-forties, strong, financially secure, and a veteran, with all the benefits that come with that honor. He could have gone anywhere and done anything. Yet, knowing about my father, he packed up his car in Fort Erwin, California, and in the afternoon of his last day in the US Army, he drove across country and chose to be with my father and mother. My brother quickly became a caregiver, maintenance man, chauffer, secretary, counselor, and friend to our parents. He saw the need and chose to surrender to divine providence. He chose to be a part of the solution rather than complaining or perpetuating the problem.

I suspect that Fr. Caussade would applaud my brother, as I do, and would hail him as an example of how we can respond to suffering and disappointment. Rather than wallowing in the mire and muck, we are empowered and enabled to stand and fight for goodness, hope, and a broader perspective of reality that lightens the sorrow and makes it redemptive.

The story of my father is still unfolding. We know that more ups and downs are coming. But I thank God for my brother's witness and for his leadership in helping our mother care for our father. This witness compels these questions: What tragedy, hurt, or harm is God calling us to, and how can we better be a witness and champion for goodness? What sorrow or suffering is divine providence permitting to which we can reflect rays of hope and joy?

We are not called to be bystanders. We are commissioned and sent. It is time to get to work!

SPIRITUAL STEPS

Some practical thoughts to help us all live the wisdom of divine providence:

- Consider the times when you passed on opportunities to speak the truth or stand up for righteousness.
- Identify ongoing circumstances that call for a voice or act of goodness. Resolve to be the one to say or do it.
- Contemplate the mystery of God entrusting you with the power of grace. It is his grace that is the solution and cure to the brokenness and darkness of our world and it is being given to you.

- Name people in your life who have stood up for truth, beauty, or goodness and have inspired you to be a better person. What can you learn from them?

CLOSING PRAYER

All-powerful and loving God,
you give us your grace and your mission.
Enlighten my mind to understand
and my will to accept these gifts,
And to use them according to your divine providence.
Lord, you have made me an instrument of your peace.
Help me to surrender all that I am to your will.
Help me to always serve and dwell in your providence.
I make this prayer through Jesus Christ,
who is Lord, forever and ever.
Amen.

Conclusion

THE LITTLE SISTERS

When I was a seminarian in Rome, I was able to meet many orders, congregations, associations, and organizations within the Church. Each of them was moved by a sense of apostolic zeal according to their respective spirituality and ministry. I was inspired. The exposure was a strong dose of the diversity, youthful energy, and sense of mission within the vast body of the universal Church.

Among the many such orders that I met, I became fast friends with a small band of religious called the Little Sisters of the Lamb. The group was founded within the charism of St. Dominic. Unlike the predominant order, which is focused on preaching and catechesis, the Little Sisters live according to the radical poverty of the great saint. In terms of their community life, the Little Sisters wear humble blue habits and live, as they describe their order, "completely on divine providence." By this they mean that they live solely by begging. Yes, by begging as religious sisters! Can you imagine a knock on your door, and when you open it up, there is a sister in full habit, begging you for some bread?

When the community is asked, "But what do you do? What is your work?" the sisters simply smile and respond, "We beg, and we pray." When pressed, they explain, "We represent the begging of Jesus Christ, who roams throughout our world, begging for the love of humanity." They then describe their extensive prayer life, intercession for the needs of humanity, and their begging missions. Each of these aspects of their way of life is powerful and introduces an examination of conscience to the rest of us.

Within the beautiful spiritual wisdom of the sisters, one of the maxims that especially stood out for me was this life-shaking declaration: "Wounded, I will not stop loving." The expression comes from their complete abandonment to divine providence and is inspired by their holy founder. The sisters pray this saying whenever they are mistreated, dismissed, mocked, or slandered. Yes, as shocking as it might seem to us, there are those in our world who treat such gentle witnesses of God's love in such a despicable manner. Yet the good sisters return love for hate, compassion for judgment, and understanding for unkindness. The motto manifests the hearts of holy virgins who live reliant upon God's fatherly care and concern for them and our world. I am confident that their spiritual work and prayers are channels of God's grace for the rest of us in the world today. I wonder how many times we have all benefited unknowingly from their quiet and steadfast surrender to God's providence.

The sisters are radical witnesses for us. So that their testimony is more credible and convincing to us, I would like to relate one story that was shared with me by one of the sisters.

The particular sister—we will call her Sr. Gloria—was traveling through small towns in South America. She and her companion were begging and praying their way through the continent. In one such town, they were warmly received by a family in their home. It was a home without a floor, no running water, and a thatched roof. It lacked much but was rich in love and joy. While the sisters ate, laughed, and sang with their hosts, an extended family member came in. The woman looked at Sr. Gloria, welled up with tears, and said, "I remember you. You're back!" Sr. Gloria was confused and thought the woman was confusing her with someone else. She replied, "I'm sorry. This is my first time here. Do I remind you of someone?" The woman shook her head, pointed to her, and said, "It's you. I remember. Many years ago, when I was a girl, you came here. I know it's you." Sr. Gloria was taken by the woman's conviction and began to rethink her own history. And suddenly, as if by a flash of light, she remembered the town. She had actually visited there many years ago as a young novice and begged alongside professed sisters of her order. She was moved by the memory and said, "Yes, my goodness. You're right. I was here."

The woman explained, "I remember you. You came here while my father was living. He welcomed you and the other sisters into our home. As you walked in, he sent me out to the market. He told me to take out credit and bring back food for you. I went but was puzzled. I didn't know how we would pay back the debt for the food. We didn't have any money."

Sr. Gloria apologized, "I'm sorry. I didn't know. We don't ask for such a sacrifice."

But the woman cut her off and said, "No, Sister, you don't understand. Up until that point, we never had enough food. Things never came together. We were always unsure where food or firewood would come from. We didn't know. But after my father made this act of kindness to you and the other sisters, we always had food. Everything came together! We knew that things would be OK. We always had food." The woman choked up as she recounted the story and concluded, "You gave us more food than we ever gave you. Thank you, Sister!"

Of course, the story transformed Sr. Gloria in her vocation and her abandonment to divine providence. She retold it as a sign and encouragement to me and to many others, of our mutual call to believe in God's care and trust in him without condition.

Sr. Gloria and the Little Sisters of the Lamb are some of a vast cloud of witnesses to us of the radical love God has for each of us. They are models and exemplars to us of the call to abandon ourselves to God's providence. While it might be expressed differently according to our state in life, we are all, without exception, called to surrender ourselves to divine providence. The sisters embody God's begging for our love. They stand as tangible voices of his invitation to each of us: "Come to me. Trust me. Give me your heart. Let me care for you."

OUR MILE MARKERS

While the Little Sisters of the Lamb never met Fr. Caussade, they are truly women after his own heart, as he also whispers, exhorts, and shouts to us about God's infinite care and eternal love for each one of us. He echoes the summons given by God in Jesus Christ, to abandon ourselves to divine providence.

In this book, we have walked through a six-day retreat inspired by the spiritual writings of Fr. Jean-Pierre de Caussade. Each day contained a portion of his heavenly wisdom. And so each one stands as a type of mile marker along our own path of drawing closer to God, seeing his presence, and accepting his providential care.

On day 1 we looked at doing our part and then leaving the rest to God. This is an important lesson for us as the future and the past are such alluring residences and often call to us to dwell there and leave our hopes or hurts in such places. Divine providence breaks through that spell and calls us to live in the present moment. It points out the importance of fulfilling our responsibilities and duties in life while also submitting ourselves to divine providence. While the temptation to worry or attempt control is strong in Western culture, our spiritual writer summons us to a healthy abandonment to the care of God.

On day 2 we explored the opportunity to embrace the present moment as an ever-flowing source of holiness. We navigated the question of time and strongly emphasized the here and now. Not yesterday or tomorrow, not there or over there, but here and now. Fr. Caussade tells us that God is only present here and now. The past is over and the future is not guaranteed. He exhorts us to find God where we are and cherish his presence there. Divine providence does not want us lost in time but truly aware and living in the abundance of the sacrament of the present moment. This practice is the heart of the abandonment to divine providence.

On day 3 we dissected the power of the present moment and elaborated on how surrendering to God is a call to practice every virtue. Rather than chasing after one virtue and then another as if in some scattered scavenger hunt, we are shown that abandoning our lives to God's care can bring all the virtues together and help us live in harmony and holiness. It is precisely God's presence and providence that attracts and orders all the virtues and their diverse expressions into the narrative of our lives. Divine providence reveals this way to us and shows us that holiness does not have to be so exhausting or troublesome.

On day 4 we dove into the intricacies of the present moment and discovered how a complete surrender to the will of God is the essence of spirituality. As with virtue, so with acts of piety. The secret is not excessive spiritual practices or a multiplicity of devotionals. If we are not careful, we could do such things, wear ourselves out, and not even grow in our relationship with God. In contrast, the abandonment to divine providence is the key to a wholesome and integrated spiritual life. Instead of disjointed pious practices or elaborate theological treatises, the message of divine providence explains that a life given to God's care is ordered by grace and matured according to its activity in our hearts.

On day 5 we underwent a surgery of the soul. Having described the different aspects of a life abandoned to divine providence, Fr. Caussade elucidates the mystery and purpose of the purgative way in the spiritual life. While not an enjoyable or comfortable time, this phase (often repeated) purifies the soul of self-love and realigns it to a deeper love and a selfless service to God and neighbor. The darkness of the purgative way needs to be properly understood and appreciated by the person who desires to live a life of surrender to the ways of God.

On day 6 we moved from the interior life of the purgative way to the active call to serve, promote, and defend goodness in the world. As God's passive will allows for evil to occur, the souls committed to divine providence are commissioned and sent to labor for the sake of righteousness. Relying on God's grace and redemptive suffering, we are summoned to work for truth and protect what is beautiful. Dismissing any sense of powerlessness in our world and refusing to allow the human family to be a victim of depravity and destruction, we are empowered to love our neighbors and suffer for the common good.

The six chapters of Fr. Caussade's masterpiece *Abandonment to Divine Providence* are small but mighty. Similar to dynamite in a quarry, they are simply wrapped but powerful in their execution. What will we do with them? Our esteemed writer has offered these lessons to us as a faithful and loving guide in the ways of divine providence. Along the way, he has pointed out, explained, advocated, exhorted, reminded, and constantly challenged us to abandon ourselves to God's providence. What will we do?

FR. CAUSSADE'S FINAL WITNESS

Fr. Caussade offers us another witness. There was an interesting turn of events in his life that is rarely recorded in stories about him or in summaries about his masterpiece. The holy priest gave the retreat conferences that became his masterpiece while ministering as a spiritual director. It was a work that he loved and from which he found great satisfaction and encouragement. Yet after some years in that ministry, his religious superiors sent him as an administrator to one of the order's seminaries.

Because he was skilled in the area of business administration and operations, he was kept in this position. He severely disliked the administrative assignment. In various letters to confidants, he wrote about his struggles and difficulties in such work. And yet even in his unwanted priestly appointment, Fr. Caussade remained true to his own teachings and daily sought to surrender to divine providence. He worked to find God in the tasks that he did not want to do, in the midst of an assignment that he did not like, and in a place that he did not prefer. Fr. Caussade stayed where he was sent, however, and died a holy death in this selfless service.

In this way, not only are the life and teachings of Fr. Caussade a strong witness to us of what can be accomplished in a soul that surrenders to divine providence, but the priest's holy death also serves as a testimony of the work and richness of a life abandoned to God's providence.

OUR INVITATION TO SURRENDER

In our retreat together, we have been led to the font of living water. Now we are once again invited to drink. We should drink such water zealously but prudently, not wasting it or delaying our reception of it (see Judges 7:5–6). We are offered a water that can well up within us and overflow to eternal salvation for ourselves and those around us (see John 4:14).

Unlike the empty promises of a fallen world that destroys itself in excessive activity, distracted thought, materialism, utilitarianism, and an ungodly rage for power and control, we are called to the refreshment of living water. In light of this prophetic wisdom, we can see the holes in the buckets in this fallen world and expose their inability to quench our thirst for meaning and purpose (see Jeremiah 2:13). Divine providence does not merely unveil weakness and emptiness. God directs us to the way of life that can satisfy our thirst and make us whole and happy. He reveals the fruits of a life that has been given over and abandoned to divine providence. God calls us to himself and to this way of abundant life.

Rather than just the spinning and toiling of life and competition, God desires to take us deeper. He wants us to have a stronger foundation and a broader spirit. Mice and other rodents can find happiness running endlessly in toy wheels without direction or value. But we were made for more. We are called to be a people of meaning and purpose. We were made to enjoy the gifts of life and to dwell in eternity forever. We are welcomed to follow the way of gratitude, awareness, and mission here and now and so prepare for the beatitude of heaven. In this way, we are harkened to exalt and rejoice in the glory and power of divine providence.

Life is not a burden or a tragedy. It is not a problem that we have to solve. We are not alone in the fallenness of our world or the sinfulness of our own souls. Life is a gift and a mystery. It is a gift that we unwrap every day. On some days, there will be joys and beauties. On other days, sorrows and sufferings. All of our days, whatever they might involve, are a part of the singular gift given to us by God's love and goodness. We are blessed to have this life, and to live it here and now. It is a mystery, but one that we are called to cherish every day through an abandonment to divine providence.

As our retreat comes to a close, we are invited to dive in. What will we do? Will we abandon ourselves? Come, dear reader! Let's not wait. Let us drink together the refreshing water of God's divine providence. We surrender!

Appendix

Here you will find excerpts from Fr. Caussade's original text of *Abandonment to Divine Providence*.

BOOK ONE, CHAPTER 1, SECTION 8

God's design imparts a supernatural and divine value to everything for those who conform to that design. All it imposes, all it contains, and every object to which it extends becomes holy and perfect, for its power has no limits. Everything it touches, it makes divine.

But in order not to stray either to right or left, we must not follow any inspiration, which we believe we have received from God, before making certain that this inspiration is not diverting us from the duties of our state. These duties are the surest manifestation of God's plan, and nothing must be preferred to them. In them there is nothing to be feared, nothing to be excluded or preferred. The moments employed in fulfilling these duties are the most precious and salutary for us by the very fact that they give us the undoubting assurance that we are accomplishing God's good pleasure.

The whole virtue of what is called holiness lies in these designs of God. Nothing must be rejected, nothing sought after. Everything must be accepted from his hand and nothing without him. Books, the counsel of the wise, vocal prayers, and interior affections, all these things instruct us, direct us, and unite us with him provided that God's will prescribes them. Quietism is in error when it despises these means and all use of the senses, for there are those whom God wishes to go by this road always. This is shown clearly enough by their state of life and spiritual leanings. It is useless to imagine methods of self abandonment from which all personal activity is excluded. When the divine plan prescribes action, holiness for us will lie in activity.

Beyond the duties imposed on us by our state of life, God may require certain actions that are not included among these duties, although in no way contrary to them. In such cases, spiritual attraction and inspiration are the indications of the designs of God. The most perfect course for those whom God is leading in this way is to add what is inspired to what is commanded, while still observing the precautions which inspiration requires. In this way, we will not interfere with the duties of our state or with what belongs purely to Providence.

God makes saints as he pleases, but they are all made according to his plan, and all must be submissive to this plan. This submission is the true self-abandonment, and it is the most perfect of all ways.

The duties imposed by their state of life and by God's Providence are common to all saints and are God's mark on them all in general. They live hidden in obscurity, for the world is so deadly that they steer clear of its dangers. This does not constitute their sanctity, however, since it consists entirely in their submission to God's designs. The more absolute this submission becomes, the greater their sanctity. We must not think that those in whom God causes virtues to be displayed in unusual and extraordinary ways and by unquestionable spiritual attractions and inspirations follow the path of self-abandonment any less. Once God's design imposes these extraordinary acts on them as a duty, they must not be content merely with the duties of their state and of ordinary Providence, for then they would not be abandoning themselves to God and his will. His will would no longer rule all their moments, and their moments would not be the will of God. They must reach out and extend themselves to the further measure of God's designs along the way that is traced out for them by spiritual attraction. The inspiration of grace must become for them a duty, and they must be faithful to it. As there are some whose whole duty is defined for them by external laws and who must confine themselves to these because it is God's design to restrict them within these bounds, so there are others who beside their external duties should also be faithful to the interior law which the Holy Spirit imprints on their hearts.

But who are the holiest among us? It is vain curiosity to try to find out. Each must follow the way that is marked out for him.

Perfection consists in complete submission to God's designs and in carrying out unfailingly what is most perfect in them.

To compare the different states in themselves takes us no further, for it is not in the quantity or quality of what is commanded that holiness is to be sought. If self-love is the motive on which we act, or if it is not corrected when we become aware of it, we shall always be poor in the midst of an abundance that is not of God's design. However, to give some answer to the question, it is my opinion that holiness corresponds to the love we have for God's good pleasure. The more his will and designs are loved, no matter what the means they ordain, the greater is the sanctity. This is seen in Jesus, Mary, and Joseph. In their personal lives, there was more love than grandeur, more form than matter. We are not told that these holy persons sought out holy things and circumstances, but only holiness in all their circumstances.

It must therefore be concluded that there is no particular path which is the most perfect one. The most perfect path is simply submission to God's designs whether in the performance of external duties or in interior dispositions.

BOOK ONE, CHAPTER 2, SECTION 1

All things exist and live in the hand of God. Our senses perceive only creaturely action, but through faith we see the action of God in everything. Through faith we believe that Jesus Christ is alive in everything and works throughout the course of the centuries. Faith tells us that the briefest moment and the smallest atom contain a portion of Christ's hidden life and his mysterious action. The action of the created world is a veil concealing the profound mysteries of the divine action. After his resurrection Jesus Christ took his disciples by surprise in his apparitions and presented himself to them under symbols that disguised him. And as soon as he had revealed himself, he disappeared. This very same Jesus, always living and active, still takes by surprise those whose faith is not sufficiently pure and penetrating. There is no moment when God does not present himself under the guise of some suffering, some consolation, or some duty. All that occurs within us, around us, and by our means covers and hides his divine action. His action is there, most really and certainly present, but in an invisible manner, the result of which is that we are always being taken by surprise and we only recognize his operation after it has passed.

If we could pierce the veil and be vigilant and attentive, God would reveal himself continuously to us and we would rejoice in his action in everything that happens to us. At every occurrence we would say, "It is the Lord!" (Jn 21:7), and we would find a gift from God in all circumstances. We would think of all created things as very feeble instruments in the hands of an almighty worker, and we would recognize without difficulty that nothing is lacking to us and that God's constant care gives us at each instant what is best suited to us. If we had faith, we would welcome all things and would, as it were, caress them and thank them interiorly for contributing so favorably to our perfection.

If we lived uninterruptedly by the life of faith, we would be in continual contact with God and would speak with him face to face. As the air transmits our thoughts and words to others, so would our deeds and sufferings transmit God's thoughts and words to us. They would be the embodiment of his words, giving them an external expression. For us, all things would be holy and excellent. While this union with God will be established in heaven by glory, faith establishes it on earth. The only difference is in our mode of reception.

Faith is the interpreter of God. Without the insight it brings, nothing can be understood of the language through which created things speak to us. That language is a cipher in which nothing is apparent but confusion. It is a thorn bush from which no one could imagine God speaking. But faith makes us see, as in the case of Moses, the fire of divine charity burning in the midst of the thorns. Faith gives us the key of the cipher and enables us to discover in that confusion the marvels of heavenly wisdom. Faith gives a face of heaven to the whole earth, and by it our hearts are ravished and transported to converse with heaven.

Faith is the light of time. It attains truth without seeing it. It touches what it does not feel. It beholds this world as if it were not there, seeing something quite different to what appears on the surface. Faith is the key of the treasury, the key of the abyss of divine wisdom, the key of the science of God. It is faith that gives the lie to all created things. It is by faith that God reveals and manifests himself in all things. It is faith that divinizes things, which lifts the veil and reveals to us the eternal truth.

All that we see is lies and vanity; the truth of things is in God. What a difference between the ideas of God and our illusions! How can it be that though we are continually warned that every passing event in the world is but a shadow, a figure, a mystery of faith, we always behave in a merely human way and judge events by our natural understanding of them with the result that they remain an enigma? We fall into the snare like fools instead of lifting our eyes and ascending to the principle, the source, the origin of things, where everything has another name and other qualities, where everything is supernatural, divine, and sanctifying, where everything is part of the plenitude of Jesus Christ, where each occurrence is a stone of the heavenly Jerusalem, where everything is a means of entrance into that marvelous city. We live as we see and as we feel, and we render useless that light of faith which would lead us so surely through the labyrinth of clouds and images among which we lose our way like idiots. Why? Because we do not walk by the light of faith which desires nothing but God and what is his and which lives forever by him, passing beyond and abandoning what is but an image.

BOOK ONE CHAPTER 2, SECTION 3

If we are able to envisage each moment as the manifestation of the will of God, we shall find in it all that our heart can desire. For what can be more reasonable, more perfect, more divine than the will of God? Can its infinite value increase through differences of time, place, and circumstance? If you are given the secret of finding it at every moment in every event, you possess all that is most precious and worthy in your desires. What exactly do you desire? Do not hold back—carry your longings beyond all measures and limits. Dilate your hearts to an infinite extent. I have enough to fill them. There is no moment at which I cannot make you find all that you can desire.

The present moment is always full of infinite treasures. It contains far more than you have the capacity to hold. Faith is the measure. What you find in the present moment will be according to the measure of your faith. Love also is the measure. The more your heart loves, the more it desires, and the more it desires, the more it finds. The will of God presents itself at each instant like an immense ocean which the desire of your heart cannot empty, although it will receive from that ocean the measure to which it can extend itself by faith, confidence, and love. The whole of the created universe cannot fill your heart, for it has a greater capacity than everything else that is not God. The mountains that alarm your eyes are but atoms to the heart. The divine will is an abyss, the opening of which is the present moment. Plunge into this abyss and you will find it ever deeper than your desires. Pay court to no one; do not worship illusions.

They can neither enrich you nor deprive you of anything. Only the will of God will fill you entirely and leave you without a void. Adore that will. Go straight towards it. Pierce through and abandon all external appearances. The stripping, death, and destruction of the senses make the reign of faith. The senses adore created things, while faith adores the divine will. Take their idols away from the senses, and they weep like children in despair. But faith triumphs, for it cannot be deprived of the will of God. When the event of the present moment terrifies, starves, strips, and attacks all the senses, it is precisely at that moment that it nourishes, enriches, and vitalizes faith, which laughs at the losses of the senses as the governor of an impregnable town laughs at useless attacks.

When the will of God has been revealed to us and has made us feel that God is ready to give himself completely if we, for our part, will also give ourselves, we experience in all circumstances a powerful assistance. From then on we taste by experience the joy of the coming of God, and we enjoy it more the better as we understand the practice of abandonment to God's will in which we should remain at every moment.

BOOK TWO, CHAPTER 1, SECTION 6

Abandonment includes all possible ways of serving God. We give ourselves up to God, and the movement caused by pure love covers the whole range of God's good pleasure. At every moment we exercise an infinite abandonment of self, and all possible qualities and manners of serving God are included. It is not our business to determine the particular matter of the submission we owe to God. Our sole business is to be ready for everything and to submit to everything. There lies the essence of abandonment. That is what God demands of us. The free self-offering that he asks of our hearts consists of abnegation, obedience, and love—the rest is his business. Whether we take pains to fulfill the duty of our state of life, or follow with sweetness an attraction inspired by God, or peacefully submit to the impressions of grace on our body and soul is no matter. In all this we exercise in the depth of our hearts one and the same general act of abandonment. This act is not in the least limited by the end of our activity and by the divine command that appears at the moment, but has in its depths all the merit and efficacy that a sincerely good will always has when the effect is outside its control. What we have wished to do is taken as done in the sight of God.

If God's good pleasure sets limits to our exercise of our faculties, he puts none on the exercise of the will. The being and essence of God are the objects of the will. Through our exercise of love, God unites himself to us without limit, mode, or measure. If in a particular case this love is determined in the concrete to the exercise of this or that particular faculty, it means that God's will also determines itself to that particular object, that God's will, as it were, foreshortens itself in the present moment, thus passing into the faculties and then into the heart. Finding the heart pure and resigned without limit or reserve, God's will communicates itself fully on account of the heart's infinite capacity actuated by the virtue of love, which having emptied it of everything else has made it capable of receiving God.

O holy detachment! It is this that makes room for God. O purity, O blessed annihilation, O submission without reserve! This is what attracts God into the depth of the heart. Let my faculties be what they will; you, Lord, are my entire good. Do what you will with me; that I should act, that I should be inspired, that I should be the subject of your impressions is all one, for all belongs to you. All, indeed, is you, from, and for you. I have nothing to say or to do. Not a single moment of my life is of my own ordering. All belongs to you. I have neither to add nor subtract, to inquire or reflect. Sanctity, perfection, salvation, direction, mortification, is all your affair, Lord. Mine is to be content with you and to choose for myself no action or condition, but to leave all to your good pleasure.

Bibliography

Caussade, Jean-Pierre de. *Abandonment to Divine Providence: The Classic Text with a Spiritual Commentary by Dennis Billy, C.Ss.R.* Notre Dame, IN: Ave Maria Press, 2010.

Garrido, Ann. *Redeeming Administration*. Notre Dame, IN: Ave Maria Press, 2013.

Hildebrand, Dietrich von. *The Art of Living*. Steubenville, OH: Hildebrand Press, 2017.

Kirby, Jeffrey. *Lord, Teach Us to Pray*. Charlotte, NC: Saint Benedict Press, 2014.

Fr. Jeffrey Kirby is pastor at Our Lady of Grace Catholic Church in the Diocese of Charleston in Indian Land, South Carolina. He is the author of several books, including *Kingdom of Happiness: Living the Beatitudes in Everyday Life*; *Doors of Mercy: Exploring God's Covenant with You*; and *Lord, Teach Us to Pray*. He has appeared on EWTN, Salt + Light television, and the BBC, as well as on Catholic radio.

In 2016, in recognition of his widespread service to young adults, he received the Order of the Palmetto, South Carolina's highest civilian honor.

Kirby is an adjunct professor of theology at Belmont Abbey College and Pontifex University/Holy Spirit College. He is also a spirituality contributor to *Crux* and a guest columnist for *The Catholic Thing*. He served in a number of parish and Catholic school positions in South Carolina. He is a veteran of the Army National Guard, for which he received several ribbons and medals. Kirby also has led retreats for various monasteries and schools of the Visitation Sisters throughout the world.

www.Frkirby.com

Facebook: fatherkirby

Twitter: @fatherkirby

YouTube: @paterkirby